Advance Praise for
The Forgotten Game

"When my favorite band releases their greatest hits album, I devour it. Years later after listening to it a million times, I enjoy the simple pleasure of hearing all the other songs and B sides. John Vampatella's book is uncovering incredible songs that weren't played on radio. If you've devoured everything Red Sox-Yankees, you'll LOVE IT. If you are new to the rivalry and era, you will understand it for the first time. I couldn't put it down and loved the historical context of each inning. I loved it."

—Gar Ryness (Batting Stance Guy)

"As a sports talk show host on WSKO in Providence and a diehard Red Sox fan in 2004, I remember that ALCS very well. While most people remember Boston's dramatic Game 4 victory or Curt Schilling's bloody sock heroics in Game 6, Game 5 was truly the unsung hero of the series. John Vampatella does a magnificent job explaining why while providing tremendous background and anecdotes that all baseball fans will enjoy. *The Forgotten Game* is an absolute must for Red Sox fans of all ages!"

—Scott Cordischi, sports talk show host

The Forgotten Game

The Forgotten Game

GAME 5 ★ 2004 ALCS
Yankees at Red Sox

JOHN VAMPATELLA

PERMUTED
PRESS

A PERMUTED PRESS BOOK

The Forgotten Game:
Game 5 * 2004 ALCS Yankees at Red Sox
© 2021 by John Vampatella
All Rights Reserved

ISBN: 978-1-64293-988-0
ISBN (eBook): 978-1-64293-989-7

Cover art by Tiffani Shea
Interior design and composition by Greg Johnson, Textbook Perfect

PERMUTED
PRESS

Permuted Press, LLC
New York ✦ Nashville
permutedpress.com

Published in the United States of America
1 2 3 4 5 6 7 8 9 10
Printed in Canada

This book is dedicated to the game of baseball,
all those who have played it from T-ball to the Majors,
and the generations of fans
who have loved the game unconditionally.
A special dedication to the 2004 Red Sox,
who finally delivered for long-suffering Red Sox fans,
who had, until that point, endured one painful experience
after another. The wait was worth it.

CONTENTS

GLOSSARY OF TERMS

AVG: Batting average. The number of hits divided by at-bats. H/AB

ERA: Earned run average. The number of earned runs divided by innings pitched times nine. $(ER/IP)*9$

ERA+: A pitcher's earned run average adjusted for the era and ballpark in which he played. Thus, a 3.00 ERA in a time when teams average four runs a game is not as good as a 3.00 ERA in a time when teams average five runs a game. The ERA+ will reflect this.

K/9: Strikeouts per nine innings pitched.

OBP: On-base percentage. A measure of how often a player reaches base safely. It is calculated as: (hits + walks + hit by pitch) / (at-bats + walks + hit by pitch + sacrifice flies).

OPS: On-base percentage plus slugging percentage. The two are simply added together. Interestingly, in this simple-to-understand metric, both OBP and SLG are weighed equally, which may not be a true reflection of their on-field value.

OPS+: OPS adjusted for the era and ballpark in which they played.

RE: Run expectancy. This calculates the number of runs a team can expect to score based on the base-out situation they're in at any moment. By "base-out" situation, we mean based on the number of outs and the position of base runners. There are twenty-four possible base-out possibilities. For example, no outs, runners at first and second. Or 2 outs, runner at third, and so on.

SLG: Slugging percentage. It's calculated by adding the total bases (1 for a single, 2 for a double, 3 for a triple, and 4 for a home run) and dividing that total by the number of at-bats. The more extra-base hits (any hit more than a single) a player gets, the higher his slugging percentage is.

WAR: Wins above replacement. This is calculated differently, particularly by Baseball Reference and FanGraphs, but it tries to calculate a player's value—using an average "replacement player" as a baseline—and taking into account hitting, base running, and fielding.

WE: Win expectancy. This indicates the chance a particular team has of winning the game at any moment. MLB.com explains that it is "derived from the number of teams that faced a comparable situation in the past and went on to win the game."

WHIP: The number of walks plus hits divided by innings pitched. (W+H)/IP

PREGAME

At 1:22 a.m. on Monday, October 18, 2004, New York Yankee relief pitcher Paul Quantrill threw an 88 mph sinking fastball toward the waiting mitt of catcher Jorge Posada, who was crouched behind home plate at a packed and boisterous Fenway Park in Boston, Massachusetts. Red Sox slugger David Ortiz, who would ultimately become known as "Big Papi," kicked his right leg and took a mighty cut. The barrel of the bat dropped into the path of the oncoming pitch and connected with the ball just above the knees. Ortiz shifted his weight and his body uncoiled, launching the ball toward the 380-foot mark in right field. Set against the backdrop of the dark Boston sky, it arced toward the Yankee bullpen.

Yankee right fielder Gary Sheffield gave chase, but the ball only needed 4.5 seconds to travel some 390 feet for a home run that gave the Red Sox a 6–4 victory in Game 4 of the 2004 American League Championship Series. FOX broadcaster Joe Buck called the play: "Ortiz into deep right field…back is Sheffield…we'll see you later tonight!"

Ortiz rounded the bases, his fist raised in the air, the crowd in full throat, and "Dirty Water" by the Standells blaring over the park's PA system. The Yankees walked off the field defeated but still confident. They had led three games to none, and as far as they were concerned, they controlled the series. For the Red Sox, however, the moment had given them hope. They were alive. Barely. But alive nonetheless.

Before the game, *Boston Globe* writer Bob Ryan had written, "The Red Sox have laid a brontosaurus egg in the American League Championship Series. They are down, 3–0…and, in this sport, that is an official death sentence. Soon it will be over, and we will spend another dreary winter lamenting this and lamenting that." No team had ever come back from a 3–0 deficit to win a postseason series in baseball. In fact, in the history of baseball postseason play going into that game, there had been twenty-five series to start out three games to none. Of those, twenty of them ended in sweeps, and only two had made it to a sixth game. None had made it to a seventh game, never mind winning the series.[1]

The night before, the Yankees had obliterated the Red Sox 19–8 at Fenway Park to go up three games to none in a series that wasn't even as close as that seemed. Game 1 had been a 10–7 Yankee win in Yankee Stadium, and Game 2 also went to New York, 3–1. The Sox had returned to Fenway, hoping that some home cooking would change their fortunes, but it was not to be. The Yankees piled up 22 hits and 19 runs, battering Red Sox pitching for 4 home runs, 6 doubles, and even a triple, hit by not-so-fleet-of-foot Rubén Sierra. Red Sox starter Bronson

---

[1] The 2020 Houston Astros came back from a 3–0 deficit to the Tampa Bay Rays in the ALCS, making it to Game 7 before Tampa finished them off with a 4–2 victory.

Arroyo gave up 6 runs in 2 innings. The relievers were not much better, with Curtis Leskanic giving up 3 runs in just a third of an inning and knuckleballer Tim Wakefield getting shelled for 5 runs in 3.1 innings. No Sox pitcher escaped the onslaught unscathed. The Red Sox had actually made the game interesting in the third by tying the game at six on a two-run double by shortstop Orlando Cabrera; but in the fourth, the Yankees exploded for five runs and the rout was on.

After the game, Hall of Fame Yankee slugger Reggie Jackson chirped, "I think it's time to break out those 'Bronx Bombers' T-shirts again. These guys are like a hurricane. Hurricane Yankee." The Sox' backs were against the wall.

Most Red Sox fans were depressed after Game 3. This was the latest in a long line of Yankee beatdowns of the hometown team. There was the Babe Ruth trade in 1920 that preceded a long period of Red Sox disappointments and Yankee championships. There was the 1949 pennant, won by the Yankees in dramatic fashion on the last weekend of the season. There was 1978 and Bucky Dent hitting one over the Green Monster in the famous tiebreaker game. There was the 1999 American League Championship Series (ALCS), which the Yankees won four games to one. And then, just one year before, there was Aaron Boone, belting a home run to left field in the eleventh inning of Game 7 of the 2003 ALCS to beat the Red Sox 6–5 and break the hearts of Red Sox Nation. Again. It was a never-ending story. Yes, it was a rivalry—but a rivalry like an ant has with a boot.

After Game 3, the *Boston Globe*'s Dan Shaughnessy wrote, "The Red Sox have been beaten senseless by those damn Yankees again, and the psychological toll threatens to shake the faith of a long-suffering Nation. How much more can New Englanders take?"

But some fans still held out hope. Ross McCabe of New Hampshire said, "Hey, we're three games out in the series, never been done before. And that's what we have going for us. The fact that it's never been done before, and it's going to start tonight. Coming back from a 3–0 deficit. We're going to win the next two here and then go to New York and spank 'em there. We're not worried yet. We've been waiting for it since 1918, it's gotta happen sometime."

Did it? It seemed like the Red Sox would never beat the Yankees in a meaningful situation. History was not on Boston's side. But that did not deter the Sox.

Before Game 4, Red Sox first baseman and erstwhile team mouthpiece Kevin Millar said during batting practice, "Don't let us win tonight. This is a big game. They've got to win because if we win, we've got Pedro coming back today, and then Schilling will pitch Game 6, and then you can take that fraud stuff and put it to bed. Don't let the Sox win this game."

The Yankees were warned. They took a 4–3 lead into the bottom of the ninth, preparing to finish off the Sox in a devastating sweep. Ace reliever Mariano Rivera came in to deliver the coup de grâce, but he walked Millar, Dave Roberts pinch-ran and stole second base by fractions of an inch, and steady third baseman Bill Mueller drove Roberts home with a single right past Rivera. Suddenly, the game was tied. Three extra innings later, the game ended when Ortiz launched Quantrill's pitch into the Boston night—or morning, technically speaking.

The thing is this. Everyone remembers Game 4. The Roberts steal is iconic in Boston history. Red Sox fans remember Roberts racing home after Mueller's single to give the Sox life, capping a seeming miracle comeback against the best relief pitcher in history. Game 4 threw the Red Sox a line, and they grabbed it.

Everyone also remembers Game 6, the Bloody Sock game. Curt Schilling, who injured his ankle pitching against the Anaheim Angels in the divisional round, struggled, to say the least, against the Yankees in Game 1 as the Yankees pounded him for six runs on six hits in just three innings. But he returned to pitch one of the most famous games in baseball history in Game 6, following emergency (and novel) ankle surgery that left his sock red with blood. In the bright lights of Yankee Stadium, Schilling kept the Bombers off balance and threw seven mind-boggling innings, allowing just one run as the Sox went on to win 4–2 to even the series.

And everyone, of course, remembers Game 7, when the Red Sox finally vanquished the Yankee bogeyman. It started early and never stopped, with Ortiz homering and Johnny Damon hitting two, including a grand slam, leading the Red Sox to a 10–3 win, clinching the series four games to three. The comeback of all comebacks. WFAN's Mike Francesa would say the next day following Game 7, "It was like going to a heavyweight fight, and all of a sudden you're just in your seat and the defending champion takes a right hand and is down for the count. The problem with baseball—in boxing you can get up and leave. In baseball they drag you around the field for about four hours. That's what happened last night. They dragged the Yankees around the field for four hours. That was a mugging...with an audience."

It was historic, and every Yankee, Red Sox, baseball, and even general sports enthusiast remembers it. Every time a team is down three games to none in a playoff series, the television network will put up a graphic citing the Red Sox' comeback against the Yankees. But few people outside of diehard Red Sox fans—and some Yankee fans who would rather have this memory burned from their minds—remember Game 5. Without Game

5, however, Games 6 and 7 could never have happened. Game 5 was the bridge between the epic win in Game 4 to the legendary series victory.

1

THE FIRST INNING

Fifteen hours and forty-nine minutes after David Ortiz
touched home plate to end Game 4, Pedro Martínez toed the
rubber for the Red Sox and peered in at catcher Jason Varitek.
Pedro had been with the Red Sox since being acquired in a trade
with the Montreal Expos back in November of 1997. Already
a six-year veteran at the age of twenty-five, Pedro was coming
off a dominant 1997 campaign, winning the National League
Cy Young Award over legendary Braves pitcher Greg Maddux.
Maddux had a fantastic season—19–4, 2.20 ERA—but Pedro
was better. In 241.1 innings, Pedro had compiled a 17–8 record,
a 1.90 ERA, and had struck out 305 batters. He earned 96

percent of the first-place votes and was considered the best young pitcher in the game.

It wasn't necessarily supposed to be like this for Martínez. He was signed by the Dodgers as a seventeen-year-old amateur free agent in the Dominican Republic in 1988 and worked his way through the Dodger farm system. His first major league action came on September 24, 1992, when he threw two innings of relief against the Cincinnati Reds, allowing no runs. His next outing came six days later, also against the Reds, but this time he got his first taste of being a major league starting pitcher. He pitched six innings, allowed four hits and two runs, and struck out seven in a 3–1 loss.

He returned the following season and appeared in 65 games for the Dodgers, almost all of them in relief. He was electric, putting up a 10–5 record, posting a 2.61 ERA, and striking out 119 batters in 107 innings. He had everything—dominating fastball, devastating curve, and a nasty changeup. He also had unusually long fingers, which allowed him to "hold" the ball a fraction longer than other pitchers, helping him generate tremendous spin and velocity from such a small frame. Martínez stood 5'11" and weighed just 170 pounds. Some in the Dodger organization worried that he wouldn't last as a starting pitcher. Frank Jobe, Dodger physician at the time, advised the team to trade him. Manager Tommy Lasorda said Martínez wasn't durable enough to be a starter and would never be more than a five-inning pitcher. Needing a second baseman, the Dodgers moved Martínez to Montreal for twenty-four-year-old rising star Delino DeShields.

The Expos put him in the starting rotation and began to make an already terrific pitcher even better. He struggled with control of his live fastball—he walked nearly five batters per nine innings in 1993—so the team switched him from a two-seam grip to a four-seam grip. The pitch became more explosive, and Pedro was able to control it better. He went from 57 walks in 107 innings in 1993 to just 45 walks in 144.1 innings in 1994, cutting his walk-per-inning rate nearly in half. In 23 games for the Expos, he went 11–5 with a 3.42 ERA.

The years 1995 and 1996 featured the development of an ace. He refined his craft and got stronger despite his small stature. On June 3, 1995, the world got to see what Martínez was truly capable of. He pitched a nine-inning perfect game but, because the Expos hadn't scored either, the game went into extra innings. He eventually gave up a hit in the tenth and was removed from the game. His innings count grew from 144.2 in '94, to 194.2 in '95, to 216.2 in '96. He was becoming a true number one starting pitcher.

Then came 1997. Pedro had finally realized his full potential. His brother Ramon, a teammate on the Dodgers, had tried to convince Lasorda that Pedro could do the job, but it wasn't enough; and so the Dodgers missed out on a generational talent. Pedro lit up the baseball world in '97, outshining Maddux, Denny Neagle, Curt Schilling, and Darryl Kile on the way to winning the National League Cy Young Award.

The problem facing the Expos was that Martínez was approaching free agency. The Expos were a small-market team with serious budget constraints. How much was a twenty-five-year-old Cy Young Award winner worth on the open market? More than they could afford. So, in the grand baseball tradition of small-market teams trading stars to big-market teams in exchange for prospects, the Expos and Red Sox made a deal. The Red Sox sent two promising minor league pitchers—Tony Armas Jr. and Carl Pavano—to Montreal in exchange for Martínez. The Red Sox then signed Martínez to a gaudy new contract worth $75 million over six years, with an option for a seventh year. It was the largest deal ever signed by a pitcher.

Pedro pitched brilliantly for the Red Sox for the six years from 1998 to 2003, and his option for a seventh was exercised. 2004 came, and Martínez once again performed well, though not quite as brilliantly as he had in the past. He was thirty-two years old and no longer quite the same. Still, a 16–9 record with a 3.90 ERA and 227 strikeouts in 217 innings wasn't shabby. In Game 5, he took the mound with the season on the line.

Yankee captain Derek Jeter stepped into the batter's box, the crowd already buzzing. Jeter was a six-time all-star in his ten-year career thus far, having won the Rookie of the Year in 1996 and having finished in the top fifteen in MVP voting five times already. His 2004 campaign wasn't quite as good as his 2003 season, but it was still all-star caliber. He had hit .292 with 44 doubles, 23 home runs, and 23 stolen bases to go along with steady defense in the field. In the first four games of the series, he had gone a modest 3–15 but had walked six times and scored five runs. He had done his job as leadoff man, getting on base at a .429 clip.

Martínez stared in and prepared to throw. Given his contract status, his declining stats, his advancing age, and the fact that the Red Sox were facing elimination, it was conceivable that, as MLB broadcaster Dave O'Brien said before the first pitch, "This could be the last time Pedro ever pitches in a Red Sox uniform." Color man Rick Sutcliffe replied, "He has just been absolutely dominating for seven years as a Boston Red Sox. Blazing fastball, devastating changeup, pitching inside, at times way inside, which is what we expect tonight." Then O'Brien: "He becomes a free agent when the season ends. His glorious seven-year run here in Boston may see the finish line tonight. And how will he go out if that's the case?"

FOX broadcaster Joe Buck set the scene: "All eyes are on the guy in the center of the diamond, and that's Pedro Martínez. He's made 31 starts against the Yankees in his career with the Red Sox, and Boston is 11–20 when Pedro has taken the mound to start the game against New York."

Boston writer Bill Simmons wrote of his feelings heading into the game, "So we showed up at Fenway on Monday in a different mood—worn out, giddy, appreciative, even a little nostalgic. We knew this was probably Pedro's last start at Fenway in a Boston uniform. If this were a Hollywood movie, he would have gone out guns blazing, the old Pedro one last time—cracking 97 on the gun, mixing four unhittable pitches and throwing at people's heads just for the sport of it. But that Pedro has been gone for a while. The older version creaks along and dances in and out of trouble, a constant tightrope walk, as nothing ever seems to come easy anymore. Watching him at Fenway, I always find myself glancing at his pitch count on the scoreboard, the same way you keep glancing at an escalating taxicab meter."

Jeter dug in, the crowd humming in the late afternoon sun, the temperature a balmy 56 degrees. Pedro delivered his first pitch, a 91 mph sinking fastball on the outside corner for strike one. Martínez' velocity was not what it once was. In the 1999 All-Star game, he struck out five of the first six batters against a loaded National League lineup, blowing away some of the game's best hitters with 99 mph heat. This was not vintage Martínez. Years of wear and tear on his arm and shoulder had stolen precious velocity. Still, 91 on the outer half with movement was not easy to hit.

"Boy, these split doubleheaders are great," FOX color commentator Tim McCarver quipped, referencing the fact that Game 4 had ended a little more than just fifteen hours previous, in the wee hours of the morning on October 18.

Martínez' second fastball was even better than the first, painting the outside corner at 92 mph. Jeter leaned over the plate and watched it sail by. A pitcher's pitch. Jeter knew better than to swing at that. Suddenly he was down 0–2, and the crowd came to its feet.

Jeter grimaced and took a couple of practice swings. "Almost a little smile on the face of Jeter as he looked out at Pedro Martínez," noted Buck. He stepped back in. Martínez delivered a 90 mph fastball on the outside corner above the belt, and Jeter only managed a weak wave. Strike three. O'Brien announced, "Good morning, good afternoon, goodnight." Game 5 was truly underway.

Third baseman Alex Rodriguez came up next. A-Rod was a polarizing figure, especially in Boston. In fact, he should have been a Red Sox in 2004. In the winter following the 2003 season, the Red Sox had pursued Rodriguez in trade talks with the Texas Rangers. He was coming off three seasons with the Rangers, where he averaged a .305 batting average, a .395 on-base percentage, a .615 slugging percentage, a 1.011 OPS, 52 home runs, and 132 runs batted in (RBI). In other words, Rodriguez had been an absolute monster, finishing in the top six in MVP voting all three seasons and winning the award in 2003. He was, simply put, the best player in baseball at the time.

The Sox had stars of their own, but they weren't thrilled with their situation. Manny Ramirez, for example, a free agent acquisition following the 2000 season, had hit .325 with 37 home runs and 104 RBIs for the Red Sox in 2003, but he was dissatisfied. Meanwhile, shortstop Nomar Garciaparra put up a tremendous season of his own in 2003, hitting .301 with 28 home runs and 105 RBIs. But the Red Sox knew they could do better, and so general manager Theo Epstein negotiated a trade that would have sent Ramirez and Garciaparra packing, replacing them with A-Rod and twenty-nine-year-old White Sox star outfielder Magglio Ordonez, who was coming off a season in which he hit .317 with 29 home runs and 99 runs batted in. It was a mega trade involving some of the sport's biggest stars.

For A-Rod, this was an opportunity to play with an elite franchise. "I thought the rivalry of Yankees-Red Sox was ripe. '03 was the year that Boston almost beat the Yankees. They couldn't. They lost that crazy Game 7 when Aaron Boone walks off in extra innings off Wakefield." He described a meeting with Epstein, saying, "I knew that they were going to win and win big. So I kind of wanted to be a part of it."

Interestingly, he had given no consideration to being a Yankee. "At the time the Yankees weren't even part of the equation. They had a great shortstop in Jeter; they had won four championships over the last eight years or so. So I was like, this is perfect. This creates kind of a Magic-Larry scenario.[2] Great for baseball, great for us, both shortstops, pretty good."

Theo Epstein said, "Manny wasn't happy in Boston and wanted out. With Nomar, it was clear we weren't going to be able to sign him past '04. Turning those two into Alex Rodriguez, who was the best player in baseball and would continue to be the best player in baseball for the four years we would have had him through the '07 season at a discounted rate—and Ordonez…was attractive to us."

In order to finalize the deal, Rodriguez negotiated with the Red Sox to take a pay cut, but the deal was vetoed by the Major League Baseball Players Association. They ruled that Rodriguez was not allowed to have his pay reduced, even if it was to facilitate a trade.

---

[2] A reference to Magic Johnson and Larry Bird, stars of the LA Lakers and Boston Celtics in the 1980s, when the two players, and their respective rival teams, dominated the NBA.

"It was like this f***ing buzzkill," he said afterward. "I think the game felt it, I know I felt it. I was saddened by it. I went out one night, there's this place called Life, and I just got toasted drunk that night. I threw up, I was so bummed."

On February 16, 2004, Yankees general manager Brian Cashman swooped in. He traded young slugging second baseman Alfonso Soriano and a player to be named later (Joaquin Arias) to Texas for Rodriguez. A-Rod waived his no-trade clause, but there was a problem to be worked out. Rodriguez was a shortstop, the best shortstop in baseball, but the Yankees had Derek Jeter, the second or third best shortstop in the game (the debate at the time raged over whether it was Jeter or Garciaparra in the number two spot behind A-Rod). Something had to give. Jeter, being the Yankee captain, wasn't going anywhere, so, even though Rodriguez was the superior hitter and fielder, he agreed to move to third base.

The Yankees had an opening at third base because 2003 playoff hero Aaron Boone had torn his ACL during a game of pickup basketball in mid-January. After the Red Sox' trade fell through, the Yankees turned their attention to A-Rod.

Epstein said, "Oh no, if Alex is willing to play third base, he is going to be a Yankee. It was like Lucy pulling the football away from Charlie Brown, the same horrible thing was happening to us again. Everything works out for the big, bad Yankees, and we were doomed."

Boston's assistant GM Jed Hoyer would later say, "My strongest memory of the whole thing was how much Alex wanted to be a Red Sox. I know everyone crushes Alex now, but in that moment in time he really wanted to win. He wanted out of Texas. I am not an Alex apologist, but he was willing to give up a substantial amount of money because he knew the contract was a burden."

Red Sox owner John Henry was not pleased. "Baseball doesn't have an answer for the Yankees," he said. "Revenue sharing can only accomplish so much [to level the playing field]. At some point, it becomes confiscation. It has not and will not solve what is a very obvious problem." The problem being that the Yankees always seemed to get whomever they wanted, no matter the price.

Yankees owner George Steinbrenner shot back, "We understand that John Henry must be embarrassed, frustrated, and disappointed by his failure in this transaction. Unlike the Yankees, he chose not to go the extra distance for his fans in Boston. It is understandable, but wrong, that he would try to deflect the accountability for his mistakes on to others and to a system for which he voted in favor. It is time to get on with life and forget the sour grapes."

The Yankees landed the league's reigning MVP, but, in 2004, Rodriguez had, by his standards, a subpar season, hitting just .286 with 36 home runs and 106 RBIs. He finished fourteenth in the MVP voting, his worst showing since he was a twenty-three-year-old playing for Seattle. The pressure to perform in New York was immense.

His bat had come to life in the playoffs, however. He had gone 8–19 (.421) against the Twins in the AL divisional round, with a homer in the pivotal Game 2, which the Yankees needed to win. And in the first four games of the ALCS, Rodriguez had gone 7–19 (.368) with two homers, five RBIs, and eight runs scored. He was bludgeoning the Sox, and Pedro knew it. He was careful with Rodriguez, walking him on five pitches, with none of the balls being particularly close.

Gary Sheffield strode to the plate. An absolutely fearsome presence in the batter's box, Sheffield as a thirty-five-year-old was still an intimidating batter to face. He pounded 36 home runs and drove in 121 runs in 2004 and finished second in the AL MVP voting. In the first three games of the ALCS, Sheffield had gone 9–15 (.600) with a home run, five RBIs, and seven runs scored; but he had been held hitless in Game 4 and was looking to get back on track early. He waved his bat menacingly as he stared out at Martínez.

Rodriguez was a threat to steal, having swiped 28 bases in 32 attempts. Despite his 6'3", 230-pound frame, Rodriguez was an incredible athlete. Pedro kept a close eye on first.

Martínez' first pitch was a knee-buckling curve that was so nasty, Sheffield bailed on it, turning his back in anticipation of getting drilled by a fastball. The ball swept away from Sheffield and over the heart of the plate for strike one.

Pitch two was a 92 mph fastball that Sheffield hacked at and sent foul behind him. It was a typical Sheffield swing—every ounce of energy went into it. He was the kind of player who made you feel like he would hit a homer every time he got up.

The crowd rose to its feet. FOX color commentator and former World Series pitcher Al Leiter noted Pedro's velocity: "This is Pedro's normal five-day rotation rest. Four days' rest, fifth day. His velocity in New York was three or four miles an hour better, which doesn't mean Pedro can't be effective. It just means he has to spot better." As if on cue, he delivered another 77 mph bender on the outside corner that froze Sheffield for strike three. O'Brien commented, "Good sharp breaking ball got him looking. Gary Sheffield walks away after a strikeout."

Left fielder Hideki Matsui dug in with two outs. Matsui was the most famous player in Japan when the Yankees acquired him in December of 2002. John Cox, the Yankee's Pacific Rim scout, said, "From our viewpoint, he's one of the few people over there that swings the bat similar to what we teach over here, and what we're looking for. He uses his hands, keeps his right shoulder in, and he's not flying off the ball like you see Ichiro [Suzuki] do." He had led Japan's Central League in OBP and slugging in 2002. In 2003, his first year in the majors, Matsui was mediocre, hitting just 16 homers in 623 at-bats. It took some getting used to the big leagues, but boy, when he got the hang of it, he exploded. In 2004, he hit .298 with 31 home runs and 108 RBIs, to go along with 109 runs scored. He was quiet and unassuming, but the lefty could mash. And he was killing the Red Sox in the series to this point, having gone 11–20 (.550) with two home runs, 10 RBIs, and eight runs scored. He was the MVP of the series thus far and was looking to put Boston out of its misery.

Martínez' first pitch was an 88 mph fastball that Matsui lifted to right-center field. Center fielder Johnny Damon glided back, but the ball kept going. He had to go halfway into the warning track to chase it down, bumping into the bullpen fence after securing the third out of the inning.

"That ball wasn't hit that well, the wind pushed it another twenty feet. It almost got out," Joe Castiglione, longtime Red Sox radio broadcaster, said on WEEI.

Pedro had gotten through one inning unscathed. It was the Red Sox' turn at bat.

MIKE MUSSINA WAS a hot commodity following the 2000 season. The then thirty-two-year-old right-handed pitcher was coming off a solid but unspectacular season with the Baltimore Orioles, but teams around baseball knew how valuable and how good he was. His 3.79 ERA in 2000 was not indicative of his true ability, as his career mark was better than that, but what Mussina did demonstrate that year was remarkable consistency. He was a workhorse, throwing a league-leading 237.2 innings, the sixth year in a row he topped the 200-inning mark. Mussina had won eighteen or more games four times by then and was truly one of the game's best pitchers.

He was a free agent, and the Yankees and Red Sox were both interested. New York signed him to a six-year, $88.5 million contract, making him the third-highest-paid pitcher in baseball at the time. Upon signing, Mussina said, "I loved playing in Baltimore, but sometimes you need to make a change. It seemed like they [the Yankees] cared more." As is so often the case, money equaled respect, and for Mussina, the Yankees had more of it to give. The Orioles could only muster $78 million worth of care, and so Mussina donned the pinstripes.

From 2001 to 2004, Mussina had performed to expectations. He averaged 206 innings a season, compiling a 64–38 record to go along with a 3.74 ERA. He was workmanlike, always professional, and sometimes elite. He had battled Pedro Martínez numerous times over the four years, including memorable back-to-back outings in May 2001. On May 24, Mussina outdueled Pedro in a 2–1 Yankee win, with both men striking out 12. Six days later at Fenway Park, Mussina allowed just five Boston hits while striking out 11, but Pedro allowed only four hits and no runs while striking out 13 Yankees, and the Red Sox won 3–0. Following that game, Martínez said, "I'm starting to hate talking about the Yankees. The questions are so stupid. They're wasting my time. It's getting kind of old. Maybe they should just wake up the Bambino and have him face me and maybe I'll drill him in the ass."

Mussina had been the winning pitcher in Game 1, following a solid opening round win against Minnesota, so he came into Game 5 with a 2–0 postseason mark in 2004. In Game 1, he had cruised through the first six innings, pitching a perfect game, until the Red Sox broke through by scoring five runs in the seventh. The last two came on a home run by Jason Varitek off reliever Tanyon Sturtze, but the runner (Trot Nixon) was Mussina's responsibility.

Johnny Damon led off for Boston and was in a major funk. He went 0–4 in Game 2 with four strikeouts, the "golden sombrero." Damon had come to Boston following the 2001 season. As he hit his prime with the Red Sox, he turned into an all-star-caliber player. From 2002 to 2004, Damon hit .288 with 46 home runs and 80 stolen bases, excellent numbers for a leadoff hitter. He had very good speed and was a terrific fielder, and he brought to the Red Sox a certain demeanor.

Mussina looked in for the sign from catcher Jorge Posada. To this point in his career, Mussina had terrific success against the Red Sox in Fenway Park. In 22 career starts to this point, he had a 10–7 record with a 3.23 ERA, which was better than his career mark. He had success in this park, he was pitching well, and his team was leading in the series three games to one. Confidence was not a problem.

His first pitch was a fastball outside at 88 miles an hour. Like Pedro, he threw harder in his younger years but now relied more on control and a variety of pitches with excellent movement. A 91 mph fastball on the inside corner was called a strike, evening the count. His third pitch was a breaking ball that hit the inside corner, but home plate umpire Jeff Kellogg called it a ball. Mussina stared in at Kellogg, unhappy with the call.

FOX broadcaster Tim McCarver said in reply to Joe Buck noting that Damon had gone 1–18 thus far in the series, "If they're going to resemble the offense that they resembled in this ballpark, Damon's got to get on base."

Damon fouled off the next pitch. Leiter added, "That's exactly right, Tim. It's not so much the batting average. Jeter has three hits for the series, batting .200, but he has six bases on balls. Leadoff…however you can get on, get on. Damon's got one walk for an on-base percentage of .105. In some way he's got to get on for the middle of the lineup." But it was not to be, as he grounded the next pitch weakly to Yankee second baseman Miguel Cairo for the first out.

Next up was shortstop Orlando Cabrera. Cabrera was a new arrival to Boston, acquired in one of the biggest trades the team had made in decades. Homegrown superstar Nomar Garciaparra, who appeared to be disgruntled and who was approaching free agency, was shipped along with prospect Matt Murton to the Cubs in a four-way deal that also included Minnesota and Montreal. Garciaparra had been considered one of the best overall players in baseball, putting up elite numbers. He won the Rookie of the Year Award in 1997 after hitting .306 with 30 home runs and followed it up by hitting .323 with 35 home runs in 1998. 1999 and 2000 were off the charts, as he hit .357 with 27 home runs, and then .372 with 21 home runs. He was on the cover of *Sports Illustrated* and was a fan favorite.

But he began to sour, and fans began to sour on him. He had always been compared to Derek Jeter, and one game in particular seemed to demonstrate the difference between the two. On July 1 of the 2004 season, Jeter made a sensational catch, hurling himself headlong into the stands to catch a pop fly. The Yankee Stadium crowd went wild, and Jeter's incredible effort contrasted sharply with images of Garciaparra in the dugout wearing a disinterested, almost sullen, expression on his face.

Theo Epstein had tried to deal Garciaparra in the off-season, and even though that trade fell through, the financial situation with him had not been resolved. Moreover, Garciaparra's fielding had deteriorated to the point where Red Sox management believed it was becoming detrimental to the club. So, at the trade deadline, Boston traded Garciaparra for Cabrera, a sure-handed shortstop, and first baseman Doug Mientkiewicz.

Cabrera had enormous shoes to fill. And he played admirably for the Red Sox since the trade, hitting .294 with six home runs in just 58 regular season games for Boston. He provided a steady presence in the field as well. He was actually one of the Red Sox' players that had a good series up to this point, going 6–17 for a .353 average.

Mussina drilled a first pitch fastball in for strike one, then missed outside with a curve. Cabrera waved weakly at a curve and found himself in a 1–2 hole but then rifled a line drive base hit to left field. The Sox had their first base runner.

Up stepped left fielder Manny Ramirez. Ramirez was one of the premier hitters in the game and had a monster season in 2004. He smashed a league-leading 43 homers along with 44 doubles, drove in 130 runs, and hit .306 on the way to finishing third in the AL MVP voting. He had been having a solid post-season so far, going 10–28 (.357) with a home run and seven runs batted in. He went 1–4 with a double in Game 1 against Mussina. He was always a threat to take one deep. Mussina would have to be careful.

The first pitch was 92 on the outside corner for strike one. Cabrera bluffed going to second on the next pitch, another belt-high fastball that Ramirez took for a strike. After a throw to first to check the runner, Mussina missed with his next two pitches to bring the count to 2–2. Ramirez drove the next pitch—another fastball—into right center, sending Cabrera to third. Bernie Williams, the Yankee center fielder, did not have a strong arm and did not even bother challenging Cabrera. Boston had runners at the corners and had something brewing.

Up came David Ortiz, the hero from the previous night's game. Buck commented, "Who would the Red Sox rather have at the plate than the guy who's digging in now, David Ortiz? Last night, four RBIs, including the game-ending home run." Up to that point, Ortiz had enjoyed a terrific series through four games, hitting .471 (8–17) with a home run and six RBIs, including going 2–4 in the series opener. And, of course, he delivered the game-winning home run in the twelfth inning of Game 4 to keep the Red Sox alive.

Mussina just missed low with another fastball on his first pitch, but on the second, "Big Papi" ripped a curve into right field. Cabrera waltzed home, Ramirez moved to second, and the Red Sox had a 1–0 lead.

First baseman Kevin Millar was next. Millar had started the Game 4 rally with a four-pitch walk off Mariano Rivera that set the stage for Dave Roberts' historic steal. Millar had come to Boston following the 2002 season, and in two years, he had become a productive and popular player for the Red Sox. He combined a fine glove with decent power and a mouth that never stopped running. Brash and outspoken, he introduced "cowboy up" as a slogan that became the team motto.

Millar worked the count to 3–2, and under normal circumstances, a manager might have been tempted to send the runners, trying to eliminate the possibility of a double play, something Millar hit into frequently. But Ramirez and Ortiz were both slow runners, and Millar was a frequent strikeout victim (91 times in 508 at-bats in 2004), so manager Terry Francona did not send them. Mussina missed inside and suddenly the bases were loaded with just one out. Yankee pitching coach Mel Stottlemyre paid a visit to Mussina.

Trot Nixon, a popular homegrown right fielder, stepped into the box next. Nixon had a difficult 2004 season, dealing with injuries much of the year. He only played in 48 games, hitting .315 but only smacking six home runs. The three previous seasons he had hit 27, 24, and 28, so the power had not yet come for him. He had gone just 4–17 thus far in the series and had produced little besides a single home run in the Game 3 debacle. He had a chance to do real damage and give the Sox early breathing room.

He may have been too eager in a moment that called for patience and looking for your pitch. He swung at the first offering, a curveball down by his ankles, and grounded it to first. Tony Clark threw home to force Ramirez, and with two out and the bases still full, catcher Jason Varitek strode to the plate.

Through the entire 2004 season, Varitek had emerged as a team leader, having come over from Seattle in a trade seven years prior. He and pitcher Derek Lowe were part of a deal that sent closer Heathcliff Slocumb to the Mariners. It was one of the best trades in Red Sox history. Lowe had become a dependable pitcher, with an occasional spectacular effort thrown in. On April 27, 2004, he no-hit the Tampa Bay Devil Rays, becoming the first pitcher to throw a no-hitter at Fenway since Dave Morehead in 1965. Only a third inning walk to Brent Abernathy kept Lowe from a perfect game. For his part, Varitek would finish his career as a three-time all-star. In 2004, the switch-hitting catcher had a .296 average and belted 18 home runs in just 463 at-bats.

Varitek had always batted left-handed against the right-handed Mussina but had suffered miserably over his career against him. He was just 4–49 with 24 strikeouts lifetime against Mussina. In an attempt to present a different look, Varitek chose to bat right-handed. "Why not?" asked Leiter on the FOX broadcast. "The other hasn't worked." The first pitch nearly got past Posada, but the Yankee backstop did a great job knocking the ball down and keeping it in front of him. On the 2–1 pitch, Mussina again missed just low, causing him to once again stare in at Jeff Kellogg. Mussina poured in a fastball to make it a full count, and on the sixth pitch of the at-bat, he missed with a slider, walking the Boston catcher. Everyone moved up a base, and Ortiz walked home with the second Red Sox run.

"Very rare to see Mussina walk in a run," Castiglione said. "He's a guy who's always among the league leaders in fewest walks an inning, but he walked Millar and he's walked Varitek."

With a chance to open the game up, Bill Mueller, who drove Dave Roberts home with the tying run in the ninth the previous night, struck out on five pitches, ending the inning. In the first four games, the Yankees had outscored the Red Sox 6–0 in the first inning, but this time, Boston had struck first and had a 2–0 lead.

It was a good start for the Sox.

2

THE SECOND INNING

"Who's your daddy?" Pedro Martínez heard this chant every time he pitched in Yankee Stadium following his September 24, 2004, outing against the Yankees. The season on the whole was a bit of a muddle for Martínez, but against the Yankees, at least in the beginning, he was solid. In his first game against the Bronx Bombers, on April 25, he threw seven shutout innings, allowing just four hits and one walk in a 2–0 victory. Then on July 1, even though the Red Sox lost 5–4, he pitched seven solid innings, allowing four hits and three runs. But September came, and two disastrous starts in a row changed the perception of Pedro forever.

On September 19, in the heat of a pennant race, the Yankees pummeled Martínez for eight hits, eight runs, and three home runs in Yankee Stadium in an 11–1 walkover. Then just five days later, the two teams met again in Fenway Park, and they lit him up again, this time for nine hits and five runs over 7.1 innings. After the September 24 meeting, Pedro said to reporters, "What can I say? Just tip my hat and call the Yankees my daddy."

For Martínez, the phrase dated back to his childhood in the Dominican Republic, but it would forever stick with him every time he pitched in Yankee Stadium, whether it was for the Red Sox or another franchise. In Game 2 of the ALCS, the chant was deafening as the Yankees managed eight base runners and three runs in a 3–1 victory over Martínez. Now, at Fenway, the partisan home crowd was up on its feet in support of their erstwhile ace.

Bernie Williams stepped into the batter's box. Like most Yankee hitters, he was having a good series, having gone 7–21 with seven RBIs. The silky smooth outfielder settled into his stance. Martínez delivered his first pitch, and Williams sent it packing into the right field stands, cutting the lead in the blink of an eye. MLB broadcaster Dave O'Brien said, "Just like that, Pedro gives one of the runs back."

Martínez had given up 26 home runs during the season, five more than the most he'd ever allowed before (21 in 1995). New York hit one off him in Game 2, and now again here in Game 5.

McCarver gave some insight into Yankee hitting philosophy going into this game. "Generally speaking, the Yankees' strategy against Pedro Martínez is to swing early in the count. Matsui did it, missed a home run. But Bernie Williams had to be looking fastball, looking for something to jerk. He got it, and did it."

Jorge Posada was next. Posada was a product of the Yankee farm system, drafted in the forty-third round of the 1989 amateur draft. He toiled in the minor leagues, working his way up until he got his first cup of coffee in 1995. In 1996, the year the Yankees' dynasty began, he appeared in just eight games. But in 1997, he broke through as a bona fide contributor. He played 60 games and showed major league power, hitting six home runs in 188 at-bats. Being a switch-hitter didn't hurt. In 1998, at the age of twenty-six, he was the team's number one catcher.

He made four consecutive all-star teams from 2000 to 2003, never batting below .268 or above .287 and never hitting fewer than 20 home runs or more than 30. He was mister consistency for New York. 2003 was his best year, batting .281 with 30 homers and 101 RBIs. He also finished third in MVP voting that season. In 2004, he saw a drop-off at age thirty-two, but he was still solid, batting .272 with 21 home runs and 81 RBIs. He was a true iron man, having played every inning of each of the Yankees' playoff games, including every pitch of the brutally long Game 4. In Game 2, he got on base three times in four at-bats and was looking to keep it going against Martínez following Williams' home run. On the 0–1 pitch, he rolled over a Martínez changeup, chopping weakly to second for the first out of the inning.

Designated hitter Rubén Sierra came up next. He was the true definition of "journeyman"—a player who played for many teams—but typically that term is used for someone who might be adequate at best. Sierra, on the other hand, was a good player his whole career. Early in his career, he finished in the top 25 in MVP voting four times, and seven times before joining the Yankees he had hit 20 or more home runs. He made four all-star teams and had hit 279 career home runs by the time the Yankees traded for him in 2003, making New York his eighth major league destination. By the time 2004 rolled around, he was a thirty-eight-year-old with some pop in his bat still, and he wound up hitting 17 home runs in just 307 at-bats for the Yankees.

He did not play in the first two games, but in Games 3 and 4 he went 4–12 with two RBIs. On Martínez' first pitch—an 87 mph fastball—Sierra lashed a single to left. But former Red Sox Tony Clark flew out to left, and second baseman Miguel Cairo grounded to first to retire the side. The Yankees had cut the lead to one.

MARK BELLHORN LED off the bottom of the second for Boston. The Red Sox had acquired Bellhorn as their utility infielder prior to the season. His main job was to back up second baseman Pokey Reese and shortstop Nomar Garciaparra, but over his career, he had played first base, second base, third base, shortstop, and even all three outfield positions. Bellhorn had a career season in 2002 with the Cubs, hitting 27 home runs and batting .258. Reese had signed with the Red Sox to be the starting second baseman, but an early-season injury opened the door for Bellhorn to slide into the starting role. Once he had it, he never relinquished it. Over the course of 138 games, Bellhorn hit .264 with 17 home runs and 37 doubles, while scoring 93 runs. From the modern metric of "wins above replacement," or WAR, his 2004 season was better than his 2002 season with Chicago.

He was in a groove the last week of the regular season, hitting .385 over his last eight games, but his production disappeared once the playoffs started. In the divisional series against Anaheim, he went 1–11 with four strikeouts. He did draw five walks, respectably obscuring a dismal .091 batting average, with an on-base percentage of .375. Still, he wasn't producing.

Things had only gotten worse from there. Against Mussina and the Yankees in Game 1, he went 1–4 (the hit breaking up Mussina's perfect game bid), but in Games 2 through 4, he was a combined 0–10 with seven strikeouts. He not only couldn't produce, he couldn't find a way to put the ball in play. Overall, heading into Game 5, he was just 1–14 with eight whiffs. Joe Buck said, "Bellhorn has had the full support of his manager, Terry Francona, while this crowd has been calling for Pokey Reese from time to time. Bellhorn, 1 out of 14, eight strikeouts in this series."

Mussina got the count to 1–2 with a sharp curve that caught the outside corner, freezing Bellhorn. On the next pitch, another curve, Bellhorn ripped a shot to the left of second baseman Miguel Cairo, who made a terrific stop, spun, and threw Bellhorn out at first. It was his first solid contact in forever, and even though it turned into an out, it indicated a possible sign that he could get it going.

Broadcaster Dave O'Brien said of Cairo, "He stole a hit on one of the few good swings that Bellhorn has had the entire series." Rick Sutcliffe responded, "Sometimes the game of baseball is just not fair. That ball was blistered, but again the New York Yankees defensively in the exact right spot." McCarver explained, "Sometimes a second basemen from a left-handed hitter will get the sign and can see the catcher. It was a curveball…leaned left, and sometimes that's the difference between making a play and the ball going into right field."

Everyone did his job on that play. Mussina executed a terrific pitch, a breaking ball down, Bellhorn got good wood on it and ripped it hard, but the Yankees defensively had him played perfectly, and Cairo made a terrific play. Top quality baseball all the way around. One out.

Damon came up for his second at-bat. Buck commented, "This guy is too good of a hitter to be held down like this." A Mussina curve missed for ball one, and then a 66 mph changeup fooled Damon and he swung and missed by a foot. Mussina then pumped in a fastball on the inside corner at the knees for a strike—the kind of pitch he wasn't getting from Kellogg in the first inning. Between innings, Yankee manager Joe Torre and pitching coach Mel Stottlemyre had had words for the home plate umpire, letting him know that they were unhappy with the strike zone for Mussina.

The next pitch was a curve in the dirt that Damon hacked at, coming up empty. The ball hit the dirt and Posada blocked it back in play, scooped it up, and threw Damon out at first. Damon was now 0 for 2.

After Damon's strikeout, FOX put up a graphic that summed up the series to that point. The Yankees' first four hitters thus far had batted .417 with five home runs, 20 RBIs, and 29 runs scored, compared to the Red Sox' first four hitters producing a .235 average with one home run, eight RBIs, and nine runs. The mismatch in the series was reflected by the disparity in how the top of each team's lineups were performing. Even in Game 1, when the Red Sox' top four hitters had four hits, three runs, and two RBIs, the Yankees' top four went 9–18 with nine runs and five RBIs (all by Hideki Matsui) as they battered Curt Schilling around Yankee Stadium.

The fact of the matter was that the Yankees had owned the Red Sox in the playoffs. Of course, the two teams had met in the 1978 playoff game in Fenway Park, won by New York 5–4, but that was officially a regular season game. In 1994, MLB introduced a radical new realignment system. Gone was the two division, two playoff teams in each league setup. They moved to a three-division setup and created a playoff system whereby each division winner made it to the playoffs. Since that led to an uneven number of teams, MLB added a wild card entry.

Before then, the Yankees and Red Sox could never meet in the playoffs. Before divisional play began in 1969, each league was considered a whole entity, and the best regular season team over the course of 154 (or later, 162) games won the pennant and advanced to the World Series. 1969 brought about division play, and that led to the winner of each division playing a series to win their respective league's pennant. Because Boston and New York were always in the same league and then in the same division,[3] they never could face off in the playoffs. That was, until the wild card format was introduced.

In 1999, the Red Sox and Yankees met for the first time in the playoffs. The Yankees had won the AL East with a 98–64 record, topping the Red Sox by four games. The Sox made it to the divisional series as the wild card entry and squared off against the Indians in the divisional round, while New York played Texas. The Yankees dispatched the Rangers in three straight, while the Sox overcame a 2–0 deficit to beat Cleveland in a series that featured one of the greatest pitching performances in baseball history, by none other than Pedro Martínez, who came into Game 5 in relief and, with an ailing back, threw six no-hit innings to help Boston advance.

So the two teams met in the 1999 American League Championship Series. The Yankees won a thriller in Game 1, 4–3 in 10 innings, as Bernie Williams hit a walk-off home run off Red

---

[3] Pre-1969, when MLB divided the leagues up into two divisions per league. In 1994, they went from two divisions (East and West) to three divisions (East, Central, and West). The Yankees and Red Sox have always been in the same division, regardless of how many divisions there have been.

Sox closer Rod Beck on the first pitch he saw. Boston took a 3–0 lead in the second inning off Yankee starter Orlando Hernández before New York third baseman Scott Brosius hit a two-run homer to cut it to 3–2. The game remained that way until the seventh, when Jeter singled home Brosius off reliever Derek Lowe. Mariano Rivera pitched two scoreless innings, pitching to the minimum number of batters to secure the win.

In Game 2, the two teams played another tight ball game. The Yankees scored first in the fourth inning, but Boston came back to score two in the top of the fifth on a two-run home run by Nomar Garciaparra. The game stayed like that until the seventh, when New York scored two runs with two outs to take the lead. Chuck Knoblauch drove in Ricky Ledée with a double, and Paul O'Neill drove Knoblauch in with a single. Once again, Rivera came in to close out the game, pitching around a couple of singles to get the save in the ninth.

In Game 3, Pedro Martínez squared off against former Red Sox ace Roger Clemens in a duel for the ages. Well, it was supposed to be that anyway. After leaving Boston following the 1996 season, Clemens had won the AL Cy Young Award for Toronto in 1997 and 1998. He wasn't quite the same pitcher, however, in 1999, posting a 14–10 record and a 4.60 ERA. The Red Sox teed off on Clemens, the raucous crowd watching their team pile up five runs and six hits in just two innings. They added eight runs and 13 hits off sacrificial lamb Hideki Irabu, and Martínez completely overwhelmed New York for seven innings, allowing just two hits, two walks, and no runs, while striking out 12 Yankee hitters. It was a dominating performance against a dominant team. But that was Pedro, after all. Or rather, it was vintage Pedro.

The Yankees won Game 4 amidst controversy, following one of the worst calls baseball fans had ever seen on a play at second base. No matter. The Yankees went on to bludgeon Boston 9–2 and win the series.

The vintage Pedro of 1999 was still dominant in 2003, the next time these two teams squared off in the playoffs. Martínez went 14–4 with a 2.22 ERA and 206 strikeouts in just 186.2 innings, finishing third in the Cy Young Award voting. He led Boston to a 95–67 record, good for second place in the division behind the Yankees, who won 101 games. Boston got past Oakland in five thrilling games while New York cruised over Minnesota, setting up the second ALCS between the two rivals.

Boston took Game 1, 5–2, as Tim Wakefield outpitched Mike Mussina, and David Ortiz and Manny Ramirez hit home runs. In Game 2, New York struck back, dealing Lowe a beating to the tune of seven hits and six runs in 6.2 innings. Back at Fenway, New York won Game 3 by a 4–3 score, as Roger Clemens (six innings, five hits, two runs) got revenge for 1999, defeating Pedro Martínez (seven innings, six hits, four runs) to take a 2–1 lead in the series. That game included a bench-clearing brawl that featured Pedro throwing Yankee coach Don Zimmer to the ground after Zimmer charged him. It was one of the uglier incidents in the history of the rivalry.

The Red Sox evened the series with a 3–2 win in Game 4, as once again Wakefield beat Mussina. Both pitched very well, but Wakefield was better, allowing only five hits and one run over seven innings. Despite striking out 10, Mussina gave up three runs (two on homers) and took a second loss.

New York won pivotal Game 5, 4–2, as David Wells and Mariano Rivera combined to allow just six hits, while the Yankees put three runs on the board in the second inning to give them the victory.

Boston came back to win Game 6, 9–6, behind the offensive firepower of David Ortiz (2–5, three RBIs) and Nomar Garciaparra (4–5, two runs). Five Red Sox relievers combined for 5.1 innings of quality relief, allowing just five hits and one run.

Then came Game 7. A game for the ages. It featured a rematch of Pedro Martínez and Roger Clemens. In Game 3, Clemens got the best of Martínez, but Game 7 was different. After a scoreless first, Boston struck for three runs in the second, first on a two-run home run by Trot Nixon, and then a double and an error brought home Jason Varitek. Boston added a run in the fourth on a Kevin Millar home run and the Sox were up 4–0. Two more runners got on, and Joe Torre pulled Clemens and replaced him with Mussina. It was Mussina's first-ever relief appearance. He got out of the inning and proceeded to throw two more scoreless frames, keeping the Yankees in the ball game. But the Sox had a four-run lead at this point, and Pedro was cruising.

Martínez had retired 10 of the previous 11 Yankee hitters until Jason Giambi stepped to the plate to lead off the bottom of the fifth. Giambi had come over to the Yankees as a free agent following the 2001 season, when he hit .342 and smashed 38 homers for Oakland, finishing second in the MVP race (the previous year he won the award). In typical fashion, as Michael Lewis wrote about in his book *Moneyball*, the Athletics could not afford to keep great players and had to win with undervalued talent. Meanwhile, players like Giambi and Johnny Damon always seemed to find their way off the A's roster and on to the rosters of big-market teams like Boston and New York. Giambi hit 41 home runs for the Yankees in each of his first two seasons but had struggled thus far in the 2003 playoffs.

He was blessed with 20/13 vision in his right eye. As a left-handed batter, his right eye was the dominant eye, and he was able to identify pitches more quickly and accurately than most players. Giambi was playing with another advantage, one that he wouldn't admit to for years down the road.

Following the 2003 season, his name was mentioned along with Barry Bonds, Gary Sheffield, and several others in the scandal surrounding BALCO—the Bay Area Laboratory Co-Operative. *The San Francisco Chronicle* wrote that Giambi had obtained performance-enhancing drugs from Greg Anderson, Barry Bonds' personal trainer. At first, Giambi denied using PEDs, but in December, his grand jury testimony was leaked showing that he admitted to using human growth hormone (HGH) in 2003 and steroids the two years prior to that.

In February of 2005, he admitted in a press conference that he used steroids. "I feel I let down the fans, I feel I let down the media, I feel I let down the Yankees, and not only the Yankees, but my teammates. I accept full responsibility for that, and I'm sorry."

Giambi would deliver the Yankees' first run of Game 7 in 2003, smashing a home run to center. New York was on the board. The game would stay that way until Giambi came up again in the bottom of the seventh, when he crushed another Martínez offering deep to center, barely clearing the fence and the glove of Johnny Damon for his second home run of the game. It was now 4–2, and Yankee Stadium was buzzing.

Boston added a hugely important insurance run in the top of the eighth, as David Ortiz homered off lefty David Wells; but in the bottom of the eighth, the game—and the fortunes of many people involved in the game—changed forever.

After seven innings, Pedro Martínez had come into the Red Sox dugout, exchanging high fives with his teammates, even getting hugs that normally indicate a pitcher's night is done. He had thrown 100 pitches and had struggled to get through the seventh. After Giambi had homered, Enrique Wilson and Karim Garcia had singled, bringing up power-hitting second baseman Alfonso Soriano, who represented the go-ahead run. One pitch, and the Yankees could be leading. Soriano fought off Martínez and finally, on the sixth pitch, Pedro struck him out swinging to end the threat. These were high-leverage, high-intensity pitches, and after 100 of them in a veritable baseball crucible, Pedro had done his job. Seven innings of two-run ball, allowing just six hits. He left with a 4–2 lead, and his teammates and coaches were congratulating him. An espn.com article wrote that "he was extraordinary, his velocity increasing from inning to inning, his fastball starting at 88 mph and eventually reaching 94 mph. Martínez had appeared to be struggling with his arm in recent weeks, but he changed speeds on the Yankees in Game 7, changed locations, moved the ball around."

After he had given up the home run to Giambi and then the two singles, ESPN's Buster Olney wrote, "Martínez then accelerated his fastball to 94 mph at the end of the seventh, finishing off Alfonso Soriano; and then teammate Nomar Garciaparra met Martínez with a hug. His pitch count was over 100, there had been some doubt about his physical condition, and with relievers Mike Timlin and Scott Williamson in line to throw the last two innings, it seemed the seventh might have been the last inning for Martínez."

That seemed even more certain after Ortiz' eighth-inning home run gave the Sox added cushion, but manager Grady Little sent Martínez out for the bottom of the eighth. He retired Nick Johnson after a seven-pitch at-bat and then faced Jeter. On an 0–2 pitch, Jeter lined a double into right field, bringing up Bernie Williams. On a 2–2 pitch, Williams lined a single to center, scoring Jeter. Suddenly it was 5–3, and the tying run was at the plate in the person of Hideki Matsui. Martínez was clearly fatigued. The Yankees were stinging the ball. Of their last six hitters, four of them had gotten hits. And the two outs that Martínez had recorded, 13 pitches total were needed to get them. He was struggling, despite maintaining good velocity.

Little had his two most reliable relievers—righty Mike Timlin and lefty Alan Embree—warmed up and waiting in the bullpen. A matchup of Embree vs. Matsui made sense from an analytical perspective and also in real time, seeing Pedro struggle. Little visited him on the mound. After the game he said, "Pedro wanted to stay in there. He wanted to get the job done just as he has many times for us all season long, and he's the man we wanted on the mound. Pedro Martínez has been our man all year long and in situations like that, he's the one we want on the mound over anybody we can bring in out of that bullpen."

Martínez got Matsui to an 0–2 count, but the left-fielder rifled the next pitch down the right field line and into the stands on a bounce for a double. It was the third straight hitter that Martínez had gotten two strikes on but couldn't put away. The Yankees had runners at second and third, with Posada—a switch-hitter—and Giambi looming.

Incredibly, Little still stuck with Martínez. And true to form, Pedro got two strikes on Posada, but on the fifth pitch—on a 2–2 count—Posada hit a double to center, driving in both runs. The game was tied, and New York had the go-ahead run at second.

Mercifully, Little finally pulled Martínez. Embree got Giambi, and then Timlin came in and retired Rubén Sierra, who came in to pinch-hit for Enrique Wilson. The inning was finally over, but the damage was done: in the game, to the Red Sox' lead; in Pedro's career, a defining moment of failure; in Grady Little's career, a soon-to-be firing.

Mariano Rivera came in to pitch the ninth. He allowed a single but got through the inning unscathed. Timlin retired New York 1-2-3 in the bottom of the inning. Rivera gave up a double to Ortiz with two outs in the tenth but got Kevin Millar on a pop out to end the threat. Tim Wakefield, on to pitch the bottom of the tenth, got the Yankees 1-2-3 as well, and the game headed to the eleventh. Rivera did his job, getting Nixon, Mueller, and catcher Doug Mirabelli in order, setting the stage for the bottom of the eleventh.

To this point, Wakefield had been brilliant, throwing 14 innings in the series, allowing just seven hits and three runs for a 1.93 ERA. He could have been the series MVP, having won both his starts and now pitching well in relief. But on the first pitch, he threw to third baseman Aaron Boone, who had come on to replace Wilson, the series ended. John Sterling, Yankee broadcaster, called the pitch: "Now we're tied at five as we go to the bottom of the eleventh. It is Aaron Boone to lead off." Fellow broadcaster Charley Steiner did the rest: "His first at-bat of the game…there's a fly ball deep to left…it's on its way….there it goes! And the Yankees are going to the World Series! Aaron Boone has hit a home run, and the Yankees go to the World Series for the thirty-ninth time in their remarkable history!"

Joe Torre said after the game, referring to the ninth, tenth, and eleventh innings, "For three innings I was waiting to see Manny turn his back and watch a ball go into the stands. It finally happened."

The *Boston Globe*'s Dan Shaughnessy wrote, "This was easily Boston's most crushing loss since the sixth game of the 1986 World Series, when the Red Sox held a two-run lead with two outs and nobody aboard in the bottom of the 10th at Shea Stadium. In Sox-Yankees lore, it certainly belongs with the 1978 playoff game in which Bucky Dent hit the three-run homer and acquired a new middle name."

The 2003 Yankees had beaten the Red Sox in one of the most incredible playoff games in history. Boston kept coming up short against New York in the playoffs, and 2004 seemed like it would be no exception, after the Yankees went up three games to none in impressive fashion. Now the Red Sox were trying to dig out of the biggest hole a team could be in. One game was out of the way. They needed three more.

With two outs in the bottom of the second inning in Game 5 of the 2004 ALCS, Orlando Cabrera lined a lazy curve into left-center field that looked like it might drop in for a hit, but Bernie Williams had a bead on it and raced in to make a basket catch to retire the side. Through two full innings, the Red Sox held a slim one-run lead.

3

The Third Inning

Not all pitches are created equal. Years ago, starting pitchers routinely threw 125 or more pitches in a game. In his famous Game 7 win in the 1991 World Series, Jack Morris pitched all 10 innings, throwing 126 pitches. In the 2000 World Series, Mets' lefty Al Leiter, who contributed to the FOX 2004 ALCS broadcast, was a horse. In two games (1 and 5), he threw 126 and, incredibly, 142 pitches over a combined 15.2 innings (17.1 per inning). In the 1986 postseason, Roger Clemens threw 134 or more pitches three times in five games for the Red Sox. In 1993 for the Phillies, Curt Schilling threw 131 or more pitches three times in four appearances during the postseason. But the number of pitches isn't necessarily the key indicator of how much a pitcher is laboring. Managers look at pitch counts plus the physical and mental toll of those pitches.

Statistician Tom Tango developed what is called "Leverage Index" (LI), which seeks to establish the pressure put on a pitcher in different circumstances. It stands to reason that an 0–2 pitch to the number nine hitter, when your team is up eight runs in the third inning, is far less stressful than a 3–2 pitch to the opposing team's best hitter, with the bases loaded in the ninth inning of a tie playoff game. The more high-leverage pitches a pitcher has to throw, the more stress is put on the pitcher. The more stress that's put on the pitcher, the more he will have to concentrate and expend physical and mental energy executing his pitches. And though these are world-class athletes, more stress on the mind and body eventually takes its toll.

Now LI, formally speaking, represents the change in a team's win expectancy (WE). This is a measure of how likely it is for a particular team (usually calculated through the eyes of the winning team) to win based on a specific situation at hand. For example, when Pedro retired Jorge Posada for the second out in the seventh inning of Game 7 in 2003, the Yankees' WE was at a mere 9 percent. When Giambi hit his second home run of the game, New York's WE jumped to 16 percent. After two more Yankee hitters got on base, their WE stood at 22 percent, ever creeping upward. Pedro was now throwing much higher-leverage pitches than he was when Giambi first stepped into the batter's box minutes before. By the time Martínez had thrown his eighteenth pitch of the eighth inning—the Matsui double that put the tying run at second—New York's WE had risen to 35 percent. Each successive pitch took a greater toll on Martínez, not simply due to the increased volume, but because of the increased stress.

In Game 7 of the 2003 ALCS, Pedro Martínez got through seven innings throwing 100 pitches for an average of 14.3 per inning. That's fairly economical and, in a day gone by, would have allowed Martínez to possibly complete the game. But in the seventh inning, he had to throw 21 pitches to retire the Yankees. And he threw another 23 in the eighth inning, thus needing 46 pitches to get just four outs. Given everything that happened in the meanwhile (New York getting seven hits and three runs), it's understandable why Red Sox fans and baseball experts were stunned to see Grady Little leave Martínez in.

Through two innings of Game 5 in 2004, Martínez had only needed 20 pitches to get six outs. But in the third inning of Game 5 in 2004, the Yankees began putting Martínez to work. Every at-bat was a grind.

Jeter was first up. Martínez delivered a sharp curve that missed outside for ball one. Then came an 80 mph changeup that completely fooled Jeter, who swung and missed. Sutcliffe, winner of the 1984 Cy Young Award after going 16–1 with a 2.69 ERA in 20 starts with the Cubs, said, "Pedro's so good at adjusting before a team can readjust to him. Jeter, striking out on fastballs his first at-bat, got a curveball and now a straight change, well out in front of it." Even with diminished velocity, Martínez demonstrated the ability to be an artist on the mound.

A fastball high and tight made the count 2–1 after Jeter leaned in and nearly got nipped by the pitch. Jeter, a master at taking pitches the other way (he won Game 4 of the 2001 World Series with a walk-off homer to right), laced a 90 mph fastball down the right field line, just foul.

Martínez liked coming inside to hitters, something the announcers noted at the start, but he also had effective stuff on the outer part of the plate. That played into Jeter's strength, something Martínez had to keep in mind. With the count 2–2, Pedro delivered another nasty changeup that caught Jeter looking, the second time he had struck out. Jeter, unhappy with the call, let Kellogg know with a few seconds' worth of discussion after being rung up.

Rodriguez was next, and Martínez started him off with a curve well off the plate. That made it five straight balls to A-Rod. A fastball way high made it 2–0. Martínez, being careful, finally threw a strike to Rodriguez, a 91 mph fastball on the outside corner at the knees. Rodriguez to this point was just 10 for 45 with 18 strikeouts in his career against Martínez, but that was normal; few hitters had good numbers against Pedro. Another fastball, this one high and away, made it 3–1. Rodriguez slashed a slider foul to the right, and the count was full. Pedro's next offering, a 92 mph fastball that Rodriguez fouled off, was waved off by umpire Joe West, as the foul ball from the previous pitch had been thrown back onto the field by a fan. Rodriguez pointed to West, then turned to Kellogg and asked, "Did that pitch count?" In the official game log, the pitch never happened, but you couldn't tell that to Pedro's arm.

Martínez was given a new ball but didn't like it, and he threw it back for a replacement. Sutcliffe noticed that and commented, "You know, when I see Pedro change baseballs, and I know firsthand, a lot of times you do that because you don't like seams, you don't like the feel of the seams on the baseball. If you want the seams, you normally are going with something off speed. With the fastball it really doesn't matter what happens with the seams."

Sutcliffe was prescient. Martínez, throwing the seventh—officially sixth—pitch of the at-bat, hung a changeup that Rodriguez sliced down the right field line. Jerry Trupiano on WEEI called the play: "Long run for Nixon, on the move, he...makes the catch!

What a play by Nixon! Went into a dive over on the side track near the wall. Came up with it, took a hit away from Alex Rodriguez. And if that ball gets by him it's a triple and maybe an inside-the-park home run." Martínez exhaled.

"What a terrific play by Trot Nixon," said McCarver, "because he had to cross over to make it. He's a left-handed thrower, this is a much easier play for a right-handed thrower, but Nixon corrals it for the second out here in the third inning. Boy, that's a dandy right there." Rodriguez waved at Nixon in disgust as he hit second base, turning for the dugout, but Nixon's effort earned him a grateful fist pump from Martínez.

Sheffield stepped into the box next. In the morning paper, Sheffield was quoted as saying, "They're a walking disaster. They act like they're tough. How they care so much about winning. But it's all a front. They're just a bunch of characters." As if the Red Sox needed any more bulletin-board material.

Pedro's first pitch, a slider, missed off the outside corner for ball one. A second slider missed badly. A curve missed outside—nothing inside so far to the slugging right fielder—and Sheffield was up in the count, 3–0. Martínez then snapped a curve over the heart of the plate, and O'Brien and Sutcliffe had this exchange on the MLB broadcast.

O'Brien: "He [Sheffield] takes the automatic, three and one."

Sutcliffe: "Yeah but normally, 3 and 0, two outs, nobody on, it's an automatic fastball. That's a lot of respect from Pedro Martínez with that 3–0 curveball."

Martínez missed with his next pitch, and Sheffield had drawn the second walk issued by Pedro. Matsui, nicknamed "Godzilla," was next. He played for the Yomiuri Giants, the Japanese equivalent of the Yankees. At the age of 28, he was interested in joining Major League Baseball and wrote a letter to each of the 30 franchises, saying, "This year, I hit 50 home runs with 107 RBIs, and my batting average was .334. I hope your team will be interested to offer me a contract for next season."

The Yankees had been following his career for years and signed him to a three-year, $21 million deal. As a twenty-nine-year-old rookie, he hit .287 with 16 home runs and finished second in the Rookie of the Year balloting, but 2004 was a breakout year for the Japanese star. Planted smack in the middle of a ferocious Yankee lineup, he devastated major league pitching right from the first two games of the year, when he went 3–9 with a home run, a double, three RBIs, and two runs scored. He kept it up all season and continued right into the playoffs.

Pedro missed high for ball one, but Martínez then got Matsui to miss badly on a changeup that dove low and away from the left-handed slugger. Sutcliffe pointed out how devastating Martínez' pitch repertoire was. "I mean, you hope at the big league level just to have one dominant pitch: a fastball. Some people have two where they can add a good breaking ball to it. This man here has three. You just saw the changeup. Some people use the changeup just to mix it in. He can dominate with that pitch."

McCarver said on FOX, "That is where a changeup is designed to be. Great motion, great location, evens the count."

A slider high and outside brought the count to 2–1, and another slider caught the corner this time to even the count. Matsui then laid off a changeup down and away and the count was full. Pedro came to the set and delivered, Sheffield breaking for second. Matsui looped a single to right, breaking his bat, sending Sheffield all the way to third. For the second straight inning, the Yankees had something cooking. Four of the last nine Yankee batters had reached base safely, and Martínez had now thrown a lot of pitches.

Bernie Williams was next. In his previous at-bat, he put the Yankees on the scoreboard with a laser into the right field seats. Now a single would tie the game. Pedro buzzed a fastball to the outside part of the plate that Williams fouled off to the left. A slider missed and it was 1–1. Martínez glanced at Matsui, a slow-footed runner who was not likely to steal. Satisfied that Matsui wasn't going anywhere, Martínez came to the plate, dropping a curve in for strike two, a borderline pitch that went his way. Williams slumped in the box in disapproval. On the twenty-sixth pitch of the inning, Martínez blew a fastball by Williams for strike three, ending the inning. Pedro's pitch count was at 48 through three innings, a pace that would likely force him out of the game after six innings.

For their own part, the Red Sox had been making Mussina work as well. In their long first inning, they forced him to throw 34 pitches, but only nine in the second (nine pitches represented a very low total in an inning). Still, 43 pitches through two innings was a lot. Both teams were hoping to get innings out of their starters, considering the abuse their respective bullpens took the night before. Boston actually led the league in pitches seen, at 3.93 per plate appearance, and they were used to making opposing pitchers work hard.

On the first pitch of the inning, Manny Ramirez ripped a Mussina fastball on the ground between Rodriguez at third and Jeter at short and into left field for a base hit. Ramirez was known primarily as a power hitter, but in truth, he was a talented hitter overall. He had a good batting eye and extremely quick hands. From 1999 to 2004, Ramirez strung together six straight seasons hitting over .300. He led the league in batting in 2002 with a .349

mark and in his career would lead the league in OBP three times (2002, 2003, 2006). If he never hit for power, Ramirez' bat would still have been a valuable asset. For his career, he finished with a sparkling .312 average. Fortunately for the Red Sox, and unfortunately for opposing pitchers, Ramirez hit for power, too.

He took his lead off first as David Ortiz came to bat. Big Papi came to the Red Sox as almost an afterthought, it seemed. In the off-season following the 2002 season, the Red Sox were in need of a first baseman. The answer turned out to be Brian Daubach, who was a replacement player during the 1994–1995 strike and therefore not a man welcomed into baseball with open arms. He had been one of the more than 100 replacement players who crossed the picket line during the strike. Tim Kurkjian wrote in the August 2002 issue of *ESPN* magazine, "It was one of the lowest points in baseball history, a time of anger, confusion and disgrace. In spring training of 1995, major league players were on strike, so teams were built with replacement players, a collection of minor leaguers, former major leaguers and anyone else who could play at all."

When the strike was over, Daubach went back to the minor leagues with the Mets' franchise in Binghamton, New York, and toiled there until his official debut in 1998 with the Florida Marlins. He signed with the Red Sox in 1999 as a free agent and played four steady if unspectacular seasons for Boston, hitting 21, 21, 22, and 20 homers, while putting up a combined average of .266 over the four years. His OPS+ (on-base plus slugging, adjusted for ballpark and the era in which he played) over that time was 111. The metric is constructed so that an average OPS+ is 100, which means that Daubach was an above-average hitter.

But he left after 2002 for the Chicago White Sox, and Boston again had a need at first base. They signed three players that off-season to fill that role: Kevin Millar (who was also a replacement player in the 1994–1995 strike), Jeremy Giambi, and David Ortiz. Giambi was the favorite to take the starting job. When Boston signed Ortiz to an inexpensive contract, Boston Globe writer Gordon Edes mocked the acquisition. "On a day when John W. Henry's successor as owner of the allegedly cash-strapped Florida Marlins sprang for a $10 million, one-year deal for 10-time all-star catcher Ivan Rodriguez, the Red Sox all but completed a winter of shopping at Wal-Mart, yesterday announcing the signing of free agent first baseman David Ortiz. While Marlins owner Jeffrey Loria said he was able to sign Rodriguez because it was 'time to step up to the plate and so I've put special money into the club,' Red Sox general manager Theo Epstein hewed to a plan that has placed thrift ahead of theatrics, signing Ortiz to a one-year, $1.25 million deal." As subsequent history would clearly demonstrate, even the respected Edes can get it wrong sometimes.

Theo Epstein was optimistic when he announced the signing: "We think, all the scouts think, he has a very high ceiling. You're looking at a player with the potential to be a middle-of-the-lineup bat in the big leagues."

Ortiz had shown some promise with the Twins. In 2001, he hit 18 home runs in 303 at-bats; and in 2002, he slugged 20 bombs in 412 at-bats. Clearly, he had power. Edes had mentioned that Ortiz' numbers in Minnesota were "uncannily like those of the departed Brian Daubach," and in some ways, Edes was correct. What Edes missed was a certain something that Ortiz had that would show up time and again during his Red Sox career.

Ortiz got off to a slow start for the Red Sox. Playing sporadically, he hit just .188 with no home runs over his first 14 games and 57 plate appearances in a Sox uniform. Maybe Edes was correct. His average improved considerably over his next 36 games, batting .328 and getting on base at a sterling .402 clip. But the power just was not there, as he had hit just three home runs over 50 games.

But a breakout game on June 27 in a blowout win over Ivan Rodriguez' Florida Marlins by a 25–8 score turned the tide for Ortiz. He went 4–6 with four runs, a home run, and three RBIs. Over his last 78 games of the season, Ortiz hit .289 with 28 homers and drove in 68 runs. Those would have put him on pace for 54 home runs and 131 RBIs over a 150-game season (a standard number of games for a healthy starting player, given normal days off). The power had started to come. His future was bright.

As a twenty-eight-year-old in 2004, Ortiz began destroying American League pitching. He hit .301 and smashed 41 home runs while driving in 139 runs. He finished fourth in the MVP voting and earned the first of seven Silver Slugger Awards. Moreover, the playoff prowess for which he would soon become famous was starting to show. In the last three playoff games of the 2003 ALCS, combined with the first seven postseason games of 2004, Ortiz had hit a combined .476 with three home runs and 14 RBIs. His OPS was an insane 1.361. In the 2004 ALCS thus far, he had hit .471 with the game-winning home run earlier that morning to keep the Sox alive in the series. Ortiz would, over the rest of his career, have many more spectacularly clutch performances.

Mussina started him off with a curveball in the dirt, then he threw a wicked curve down in the zone that Ortiz swung at and missed. He dropped in another curve for a called strike and then threw yet another one that Ortiz missed by six inches for the strikeout. Four pitches, four curveballs, and Ortiz was gone. Not a single fastball.

Millar was next and jumped all over a first-pitch fastball, lining it foul into the stands. After a fastball high and outside,

Millar softly hit the next pitch—breaking his bat in the process—to Jeter at short. It looked like a possible double-play ball, but the ball hit just past where the grass and the dirt meet, causing an awkward bounce, and hit him in the heel of the glove and hand placed just above his glove, then his chest, and ricocheted away. It was not an easy play, but one that Jeter should still have made. Everyone was safe. Instead of an inning-ending double play, the Sox suddenly had two runners on with just one out.

"An error by Jeter," O'Brien said on the MLB broadcast. "A rare mistake from the Yankee captain. Runners safe at first and second."

It was, in fact, Jeter's second error of the series, and third of the postseason. He would win the first of five Gold Glove Awards in 2004 for his usual steady play in the field. What would be problematic for Jeter as the years would go on would be his range, dropping every year, as he lost quickness. Balls he could get to as a twenty-two-year-old suddenly were out of reach in his thirties. "Past a diving Jeter" became a refrain.

But handling balls he could reach generally was not a problem. In 2004, his fielding percentage was .981, better than the league average of .972. Jeter was sure-handed, so making two errors in five games was not normal. But the fact was that Rodriguez, aside from being a much better hitter than Jeter, was also a much better fielder at shortstop, too. For example, from 2000 to 2003, Jeter's fielding percentage at shortstop was .970. In those same four years, playing the same position, Rodriguez put up a .984 fielding percentage. A deeper dive into the world of advanced metrics shows that Rodriguez not only was better at fielding balls he could get to, but his overall defense saved more runs than Jeter. The metric, called "Total Zone Total Fielding Runs Above Average" (a cumbersome term usually abbreviated as

Rtot), takes range and fielding into account and measures players' defense compared to the "average" player. It measures the total number of runs above or below average a player is worth based on the number of plays made. In those four years, Jeter never had a positive number, indicating that he was below average overall defensively. Defensively, he was worth -72, meaning he was 72 runs worse than average over a four-year period. Rodriguez, on the other hand, was at +16. So the difference between the two players over a four-year period was 88, or 22 runs a year. That's a colossal gap between the two.

The long story short is that Rodriguez made a huge sacrifice by moving to third base. Jeter had made it clear that he was not moving from shortstop, and the Yankees had a hole at third base. If one was interested merely in maximizing the players' strengths, the absolute correct move for New York would have been to move Jeter to third and put A-Rod at short. Chris Mitchell, writing for "Pinstripe Alley" in 2014, citing other advanced metrics like UZR ("zone rating," which measures fielders' success in turning balls hit into their fielding "zones" into outs), made the case for Rodriguez:

"Jeter's bat was a key cog in the Yankees' lineup during the dynasty era, but he gave much of that value back on the other side of the ball. His offense was worth 163 runs above average from 1996–2001, but he was 66 runs worse than the average short-stop. After adjusting for position, that made him roughly 20 runs worse than the average fielder....Per UZR, A-Rod was the best shortstop in baseball from 2002–2003, putting up an impressive +24 UZR—leaps and bounds better than Jeter's -4 mark. On defense alone, A-Rod was worth something like two wins more than Jeter before he made the switch to the hot corner."

When Rodriguez signed with New York, general manager Brian Cashman knew there would be all sorts of questions about which player would play where. In a telephone news conference, he said, "It's not a consideration whatsoever [referring to Rodriguez playing short and moving Jeter elsewhere]. You go with the man who brought you to the dance. You don't mess with success. I'd like to take the time to put this all to rest right now. This move would not have happened if Alex Rodriguez had not agreed to move and play third base. Otherwise, we would not even consider it. I stress the fact that there is no issue. No, 'Who's the quarterback?'"

Over the years, the relationship between Jeter and A-Rod soured. Ryan Bort, writing for *Newsweek* in 2017, observed, "After Jeter glared at A-Rod following a missed pop fly in 2006, general manager Brian Cashman had to step in and remind the shortstop that everyone can see his resentment. Cashman also told Jeter to 'fake' a congenial relationship with Rodriguez. So acrimonious were Jeter's feelings toward A-Rod that the Yankees were afraid to even broach the subject with him. 'It would've been the last conversation I ever had with Derek,' a Yankee official said in *The Captain*. 'I would've been dead to him. It would've been like approaching Joe DiMaggio to talk to him about Marilyn Monroe.'"

Tom Verducci of *Sports Illustrated* wrote at the time, "How, for instance, will Rodriguez, 28, and Jeter, 29, coexist? Both are signed through 2009 with no-trade clauses; the superior defender of the two, Rodriguez, will play out of position; and their friendship has been strained since A-Rod's critical comments about Jeter in an '01 magazine interview. 'Everybody knows their best lineup would be A-Rod at short and Jeter at second,' one American League manager says, 'but it won't happen because it's Jeter's team.'"

Tyler Kepner of the *New York Times* wrote at the time of the signing, "[Yankees owner] Steinbrenner and general manager

Brian Cashman have both spoken to Jeter to assure him he will stay at shortstop, even though Rodriguez has won two Gold Gloves there and Jeter has none. On a conference call yesterday, Cashman essentially roped off the area around shortstop and put up a 'Keep Out' sign for Rodriguez."

David Waldstein would write in a 2020 *New York Times* article, "Among the many traits that combined to make Derek Jeter one of the most admired and adored baseball players of his generation, there was talent, drive and focus—and a good dose of stubbornness, too. Opposing pitchers felt it, even when they had great stuff. If they found a way to beat him on a Friday, Jeter figured out a way to respond by Saturday. Backups of his with high aspirations saw it, too. For virtually all of his twenty-year career, Jeter clung stubbornly to that shortstop position, molding it into one of the highest-profile jobs in sports, like quarterback of the Dallas Cowboys or striker for Barcelona. Even when a superstar like Alex Rodriguez, the best shortstop in baseball, joined the team in 2004, he would be the one to move to third base. Jeter was staying put, because he was stubborn enough to believe that he was the best person to be at shortstop for the Yankees, a dirt kingdom he stamped as his own and guarded tenaciously."

So Rodriguez, the superior fielder, was put at third, and Jeter remained at short. And instead of turning a double play on the Millar grounder, his error allowed Ramirez to reach second safely, and Millar to reach first, and suddenly the Red Sox were threatening.

Trot Nixon, who made the great catch in the top of the inning, came up with a chance to widen the Red Sox' lead. But Mike Mussina wasn't one of the better pitchers in baseball for no reason. A true pro, Mussina bore down. He quickly went up 0–2 to Nixon on a sharp curve and a changeup. Then Mussina buried a 91 mph fastball in on Nixon, who swung and missed for the second out. Three pitches, three strikes, and Nixon headed back to the dugout.

Varitek was up again, batting right-handed for the second time. He fouled the first pitch off for a strike. Buck commented on Varitek's experiment: "This is like grabbing a driver in the pro shop and going to play in the club championship, having not hit it before. Here's Varitek, with his team facing elimination in Game 5, just testing out something new against Mike Mussina with the hope that it might work."

He chopped a curve foul and fell behind no balls and two strikes. Mussina then froze Varitek with a curve that hit the inside corner. Varitek knew it and simply started walking toward the dugout before Kellogg even started ringing him up. Mussina had gotten out of the jam, and the Yankees were coming up down 2–1.

4

THE FOURTH INNING

The game entered the middle innings, or at least what would normally be considered the middle innings of a standard nine-inning game. In modern playoff baseball, if a starter gets to the middle innings[4] and runs into trouble, often the manager will

---

[4] In Game 6 of the 2020 World Series, Blake Snell of Tampa Bay was cruising into the sixth inning. Through five innings, he had allowed just one hit and no runs, walking nobody and striking out nine Dodgers. But he gave up a one-out single to LA's number nine hitter, and manager Kevin Cash promptly pulled him. Snell had only thrown 73 pitches, but Tampa Bay's philosophy was to not let pitchers see hitters for a third time. Reliever Nick Anderson promptly blew the lead, and LA went on to win 3–1 to clinch the World Series. Moreover, starters are often pulled in the playoffs if they get in a little trouble in the early innings, too. In Game 4 of the 2018 American League Division Series, Yankee manager Aaron Boone pulled starter C. C. Sabathia after just three innings, when Sabathia gave up three runs. His replacement, Zach Britton, gave up a leadoff home run to Christian Vazquez, which proved to be the winning run.

pull him in favor of what would become a string of relief pitchers. Numerous studies have been done on pitchers' effectiveness as they face the batting order for a second, third, and even fourth time. Most pitchers' effectiveness lessens with each successive time through the lineup for two reasons. First, fatigue; by the time they face hitters for a third time, by definition they've thrown more pitches, which means more stress on the arm and more emotional and physical wear and tear. Second, hitters have had a chance to see what the pitcher has in terms of velocity, command, and movement and have at least one at-bat's worth of seeing how the pitcher will approach them; and so they have a better chance to adjust as the game goes along.

Consider Alex Rodriguez. A great hitter, he was no different in this regard. His career batting average was .300 against starters, .285 against relievers. His OPS against starters was .945 but just .899 against relievers.

When you break it down even further, you see the effect of seeing a pitcher multiple times. A-Rod's batting average and OPS against starters the first time he saw them were .282 and .908, the second time were .303 and .936, and the third time were .317 and 1.003. Interestingly, they dropped off again the fourth time, but that could be chalked up to a small sample size of just 349 career fourth at-bats against a starter in his entire 2,784 game career (or once every eight games). When facing a reliever for the first time, he hit .280 with an .886 OPS, and in the mere 249 plate appearances against a reliever for the second time, the numbers rose to .363 and 1.081.

The OPS+ for all hitters facing a pitcher for the first time is 91, which is below average (100 is average). It jumps to 101 the second time, and then reaches an impressive 117 the third time. From a pitching perspective, their average ERA goes from 4.08

facing a lineup the first time through to 4.20 the second time, and 4.57 the third time.

These numbers have caused modern managers to exercise extreme caution with starting pitchers, especially during playoff games. Only the elite starting pitchers get a long enough leash to face hitters three or four times in most recent years. In 2004, however, managers tended to still ride their starting pitchers as long as they could. Pedro Martínez wasn't vintage, but he was still someone that Terry Francona wanted on the mound as long as possible.

Pedro presented an interesting counterexample to the data above. In 2004, he tended to get better as the game wore on. Facing a lineup for the first time, he held opponents to a .743 OPS; the second time through, it dropped to .688; and the third time through, it fell all the way down to .651. The fourth time through, however, the number rose dramatically, to .809. Pedro had so many quality pitches that he could set hitters up for future at-bats, which is one reason he had success as the game wore on. But at a certain point, given the effort he put into each pitch, fatigue would set in and his effectiveness would drop off considerably. In his postseason career, Pedro held hitters to a .189 batting average through 100 pitches. But from pitches 101 and beyond, their average skyrocketed to .391. Finding just the right time to pull him was critical. In 2003, Grady Little grossly miscalculated. Would Francona figure it out?

On the FOX broadcast, Buck mentioned the rising pitch count and said, "Terry Francona will be forced at some point in this game to try [and] extend Pedro Martínez to take some of the load off that bullpen that had to work so long last night." McCarver replied, "So his two options are to go way over 100 pitches with Pedro Martínez, and risk inefficiency there, or go to the bullpen. Both are not viable options."

The night before, the three key members of the Red Sox' bullpen had to put in extended work to keep Boston alive. Mike Timlin had thrown 37 pitches, Keith Foulke 50, and Alan Embree 30 in the meat grinder that was Game 4. Additionally, Curtis Leskanic and Mike Myers threw 13 and 4 pitches, respectively, but they were either specialists (in the case of Myers) or the last man in the bullpen (in the case of Leskanic), and Francona did not want to have to utilize either pitcher that much.

Jorge Posada grounded Martínez' first pitch between first and second for a base hit to start the inning. Martínez then missed twice to Rubén Sierra before getting a strike on a slider. Sierra fouled the next pitch back to even the count at 2–2. Pedro tried to get Sierra to chase a changeup, but it was too high and outside, and Sierra didn't bite. The count was full. On the 3–2 pitch, Pedro once again missed with a changeup, and Sierra drew the walk, moving Posada to second. The Yankees had two on and nobody out.

Tony Clark was next. Clark broke into the major leagues in 1995 with Detroit at the age of twenty-three. He played sparingly, appearing in 101 at-bats over the span of 27 games. He did not play enough to qualify for rookie status, so his official rookie campaign was the following season in 1996. He played very well for a rookie, hitting .250, but homering 27 times in just 376 at-bats. At 6'8" tall, he gave infielders a huge target to throw to. He finished third in the Rookie of the Year voting.

His prime came over the next three seasons, where he hit a combined .282, with a .365 on-base percentage and a 125 OPS+, and jacked 97 homers while driving in 319 runs. He had become a legitimate middle-of-the-order bat for a quality team. The next year, the injuries began. In 2000, he only played 60 games, and then 126 in 2001. In those 186 games, he hit fewer home runs

(29) than he had in any of the three previous seasons, though his doubles production made up for it, and his OPS+ remained high.

Detroit put him on waivers after the 2001 season, and Boston picked him up and paid him $5 million for the 2002 season. His debut was terrific, going 3–5 with a home run, three RBIs, and two runs scored. But that would represent the high-water mark of the season for Clark. His average plummeted to .146 by mid-April, and as of June 2, it stood below the "Mendoza Line" (named for Mario Mendoza of the 1979 Mariners as a joke on the weak-hitting shortstop's average that hovered around .200) at .197. Moreover, his power had disappeared. By season's end, he had played only 90 games, hitting .207 with a .265 on-base percentage and a pathetic .556 OPS. He managed to hit only three home runs all season. In his last 31 games, he hit .171 with no home runs and a pathetic two runs batted in.

It was a disastrous season in every way for Clark, and Boston let him go. He found a new home with the New York Mets and promptly rediscovered his power stroke, hitting 16 home runs in 254 at-bats. From there, he joined the Yankees in 2004 as a bench player behind Jason Giambi and John Olerud. In 106 games, he managed to hit 16 more home runs over 253 at-bats and served as a helpful player. In the ALCS, he was forced into action for Games 3 and 4 as Giambi and then Olerud were out with injuries and had gone 2–8. He came up here with two runners on and nobody out. Pedro dispatched him on four pitches, the last one a particularly nasty change that Clark swung at and missed badly. It would not be the last time in the game—or series—that Clark would come up in a huge spot.

Miguel Cairo was next. So often, teams that make it deep into the playoffs in baseball are helped in no small part by players who have out-of-the-ordinary seasons. Guys step up when they weren't expected to, perhaps playing a larger role than anticipated or having a career year. Cairo was just that for the 2004 Yankees. From 1996, his first taste of the majors, to 2003, he played for four different teams. He would play for nine over the course of his seventeen-year career. Toronto, Chicago (Cubs), Tampa Bay, and St. Louis—all cities he called home.

He was never an all-star, and rarely a starter. In only four seasons did he even play 119 or more games or get 350 or more at-bats. He never hit more than .295 in any single season and never hit more than eight home runs in a season. And at no point did he ever post an OPS+ of 110 or greater over the course of a season.

But what Cairo did was play a lot of different positions. Over the course of his career, he played first base, second base, third base, shortstop, left field, and center field. At the start of the season, Enrique Wilson was the starter, and in three of his first four appearances, and in five of his first eight, Cairo came in as a late-inning defensive replacement. But he played well in the time he was given, and by April 27, he was hitting .308. Wilson, meanwhile, was struggling, posting a .167 average by April 27. From that point on, the roles switched, and Cairo was the primary starter, with Wilson assuming the role of utility infielder, backing up second and occasionally shortstop. Cairo played even better as the season went along, and in September and October, he hit .349 with a .901 OPS over 29 games. He was also a key in many Yankee victories. In games the Yankees won, Cairo hit .310 with an .817 OPS, and in losses, he hit just .250 with a .642 OPS. For the season, Cairo would hit .292, with six homers and 42 RBIs. His 100 OPS+ gave the Yankees one of the best number nine hitters in all of baseball.

He had a chance to deliver for New York here in the fourth, and he took Martínez deep into the count. On the 3–1 pitch, the runners broke, but Cairo fouled the pitch back. He did not strike out much, so Joe Torre had confidence that he would keep them out of a "strike-em-out, throw-em-out" double play. They ran again on the 3–2 pitch, and Cairo hit a routine pop fly to right field that Trot Nixon handled easily.

Now there were two outs, and neither Clark nor Cairo had managed to advance the runners. Jeter was next, and Buck said, "Jeter is waiting to put his stamp on this ALCS." But on the first pitch, he swung and hit a one-hopper to Millar at first, who tossed underhand to Martínez covering, and Pedro was out of the inning. That would be classified as a squander, as a team of this caliber should be expected to put at least one run across if the inning started with runners at first and second with nobody out. But they failed, letting Martínez off the hook. Still, he did throw another 18 relatively high-stress pitches.

In the bottom of the inning, Boston had the 8-9-1 hitters up: Mueller, Bellhorn, and Damon.

If Cairo represented the Yankee veteran who would have a surprisingly good year to help his team reach deep into the play-offs, Bill Mueller was his Boston equivalent—and then some. He played the first five seasons of his MLB career with the San Francisco Giants, always a solid, steady player. He was a fifteenth-round selection by the Giants in 1993 and worked his way to the majors as a twenty-five-year-old in 1996. In November of 2000, the Giants traded him to the Cubs for right-handed reliever Tim Worrell, and he played nearly two seasons for the Cubs, once again performing solidly. Then in September of 2002, the Cubs traded him back to the Giants, this time for the immortal Jeff Verplancke. Mueller did not play much, but the Giants made it all the way to the World Series that season, losing to the Angels in seven games. He became a free agent after the season, and Boston signed him to play third base for the 2003 season.

He proceeded to have a career year for Boston, hitting .326, getting on base at a .398 clip, and providing the best power numbers of his career, hitting 45 doubles and 19 home runs. He finished twelfth in the AL MVP voting, the only time in his career that he would have any MVP consideration.

Boston, of course, lost in seven games to the Yankees in the ALCS that year, but Mueller was back for the 2004 campaign. He didn't perform at the same lofty standards, but he was still very good, hitting .283 with 12 home runs and 27 doubles in just 110 games. On July 24, he hit a two-run home run off Mariano Rivera in the bottom of the ninth inning to give Boston a memorable and dramatic 11–10 victory. That game featured a brawl involving Varitek and Rodriguez, with Varitek shoving his glove in Rodriguez' face. The game represented a turning point for Boston, as they were 52–44 (.542) before that game and 46–20 (.697) from that point on.

Mueller was a much better hitter at Fenway Park than on the road. In 2004, he hit .344 with a .993 OPS at home and just .225 with a .638 OPS on the road. He also saved his best performances for the Yankees. Against New York that season, Mueller hit a sparkling .333, with a .407 on-base percentage and a 1.113 OPS. In just 13 games, he hit five home runs, four doubles, scored nine runs, and drove in 13. He was a one-man Yankee wrecking crew. And, of course, in Game 4 the previous night, he delivered Dave Roberts from second base with a single to center field in the ninth inning, tying the game and giving Boston a chance to win.

On the second pitch of the at-bat, Mueller drove a fly to deep left center. Bernie Williams raced over and made a catch at the warning track in front of the Green Monster. Mueller had given it a ride but came up a little short.

Bellhorn was next, still looking to get on track. Buck said, "Bases empty for Bellhorn, who, if nothing else, hit the ball sharply his first time up. Took a good play by Cairo to his left to rob him of a hit." O'Brien said, "Mark Bellhorn now, trying to get off the schneid. One for 15 in the series, 0 for 1 tonight." He quickly fell behind 0–2 after Mussina got a generous call on the outside corner for the second strike. Mussina tried to get him to chase twice and missed, drawing the count to 2–2. He then ripped a line drive right at Cairo, who was positioned perfectly again, and he caught it for the second out. Bellhorn—who would have his moments of glory later in the series—continued to make outs.

Damon came up, still struggling at 0 for 2. Mussina led him off with a fastball outside, followed by another fastball outside that was called a strike by Kellogg. The conversation Joe Torre and Mussina were having with Kellogg early on might have been paying off, as this was the second pitch of the inning that was off the plate but called a strike. Damon chopped one foul to fall behind 1–2. Mussina threw a curve low and away, and Damon slashed it foul into the third base stands. Another foul ball allowed Damon to stay alive, still 1–2. Mussina missed with another curve but then fooled Damon with a wicked changeup, Damon swinging and missing badly for strike three to end the fourth inning. Six of the last ten Red Sox outs were by way of the strikeout. Mussina was settling in and gaining control of the game.

5

THE FIFTH INNING

Pedro Martínez took the mound in the fifth, ready to face the 2-3-4 hitters in the fearsome Yankee lineup: A-Rod, Sheffield, and Matsui. These three represented the thunder in New York's offense. They combined for 338 runs scored, 196 extra base hits, 113 home runs, and 335 runs batted in over the course of the 2004 season. Through the first eight games of the 2004 playoffs, the three sluggers had combined to go 52–111 (.468 average), with 31 runs scored, 15 doubles, 1 triple, 8 home runs, and 28 RBIs. Absolutely monster production from this trio.

It was a daunting gauntlet for any pitcher to face. But Pedro Martínez was not just any pitcher. He was, during his peak seasons from 1997 to 2003, simply the greatest pitcher the sport had (or still has) ever seen. That may seem like a grandiose claim to make on behalf of the slender right-hander, but one must understand what his staggering numbers represent.

Any conversation about the "greatest" must, of course, take into context the era in which any athlete played. Generally speaking, a list of the best pitchers in baseball history includes these names: Walter Johnson, Grover Cleveland Alexander, Christy Mathewson, Sandy Koufax, Mordecai "Three Finger" Brown, Cy Young, Greg Maddux, Randy Johnson, Tom Seaver, Lefty Grove, Roger Clemens, Tim Keefe, Bob Gibson, Clayton Kershaw, Warren Spahn, Mariano Rivera, and Pedro Martínez.[5] There is a pretty clear cluster of pitchers that belong in the ancient history wing of the pitchers' inner circle: Johnson, Young, Alexander, Mathewson, Brown, and Keefe. There was nothing wrong with these pitchers. They were legendary and put up staggering numbers. For example, consider Keefe's 1883 season with the New York Metropolitans. He threw an unfathomable 619.0 innings, winning 41 games, and striking out 359 batters, while posting a 2.41 ERA. Now let's be clear: 619 innings is absolutely absurd, by any measure. Back then, they played anywhere from four to six games in a given week, and the season went from May 1 through September 29. It wasn't quite as packed as the modern 162-game schedule, but nonetheless, it was certainly busy enough. What's interesting is that the Metropolitans only had 12 players on the entire roster, and 10 of them were position players—eight starters and two substitutes. And they only had two pitchers.

---

[5] You might be shocked to not find Nolan Ryan on this list. To be sure, he was an all-time great, and nobody has come close to his seven no-hitters or career-best 5,714 strikeouts. But as great as Ryan was, he only had one season with an ERA+ of better than 142, and he never won a single Cy Young Award. He was great, just not on the short list of the truly all-time greatest.

Two. Not two starters. Two pitchers. Total. As a team, the Metropolitans pitched 874 innings. Keefe threw 619 of them, and Jack Lynch threw the other 255. Keefe pitched 68 games, all of them complete games, over the span of five months, meaning he pitched an unfathomable 30 innings a week. Basically two out of every three games they played, Keefe threw a complete game.

There is absolutely no way the human body can do that if maximum effort is being employed. Keefe pitched 400+ innings a staggering seven times in his career. Ten times he threw 300+ innings. It wasn't as if he performed this herculean feat once and never came close again. In 1886, he threw 535 innings and won 42 games.

The game was simply a different animal back then. As a team, the Metropolitans hit a grand total of six home runs the entire season. The best hitting team in the league at the time was the Cincinnati Red Stockings, who hit .262 with 34 home runs as a team.

The "dead ball era" lasted until the arrival of Babe Ruth. Before then, pitchers like Keefe and Cy Young and Walter Johnson pitched an obscene amount of innings, with ridiculously low earned run averages, mainly because the ball was constructed in a way as to make it nearly impossible to drive to deep parts of the field. Games were played with just one baseball that took a beating over the course of a game and got scuffed up in the process. Pitchers discovered that scuffed baseballs had more movement, and doctoring the ball was legal anyway. The spitball was allowed. In 1908, teams averaged a mere 3.4 runs a game. It was incredibly difficult to drive the baseball and score runs. Teams had to manufacture runs by bunting, stealing bases, and employing other tactics to get on base, move runners over, and get them in. Pitchers simply did not have to work as hard during this period.

This is not to say that Young, Johnson, Keefe, et al., weren't great pitchers. They were. But in the context of history, it's difficult to picture them holding a candle to the greats of modern times. Imagine a Randy Johnson, throwing 99 miles an hour with a nasty slider, also able to scuff up the ball as he wished, and pitching a ball that got abused over the course of the game and was "soft" by manufacture. It is hard to fathom many runs being scored off the Big Unit.

The list therefore shrinks, removing the dead ball pitchers from the equation. The next cluster includes Spahn, Seaver, Gibson, Koufax, and Grove. Grove pitched from 1925 till 1941, a wonderful stretch of baseball against some incredible competition. He led the league in strikeouts per nine innings five times in his first six seasons, and his best years featured a season (1931) in which he went 31–4 with a 2.06 ERA. He was a marvelous pitcher who would finish with 300 wins against just 141 losses. But Grove also competed before integration and so missed out going up against some of the best players in the world, who just happened to be playing in the Negro Leagues. He also never had an ERA under 2.00 for a single season. Grove, as great as he was, misses the cut in the "greatest of all time" conversation.

Spahn entered the league just after Grove left and in his own right was a phenomenal pitcher. He won 363 career games, led the league in strikeouts four times, and won 20+ games in six straight seasons. He pitched most of his career after baseball was integrated, and from 1954 to 1964, he played with the immortal Hank Aaron for the Milwaukee Braves (the team moved from Boston following the 1952 season). He won 20 games 13 times over the course of his legendary career and was one of the best winners the sport has ever seen.

But Spahn simply wasn't as dominant as other pitchers on the list. Like OPS+, there is a metric called ERA+, which measures a pitcher's earned run average (earned runs allowed per nine innings) against his peers, given the time period in which they performed, the ballparks they pitched in, etc. In the dead ball era, some of the parks had fences more than 500 feet away. Conversely, the right field fence at old Ebbets Field was just 297 feet away. Pitching in cavernous Huntington Avenue Grounds (home of the Red Sox before Fenway Park was built), which featured a center field fence some 635 feet from home plate, is a completely different animal from pitching in tiny Ebbets Field.[6] Like with OPS+, a 100 score represents an average ERA+, and anything above that is better than average, while anything below is, well, below average. Pitchers who start putting up ERA+ numbers above 150 are truly excellent. Anything over 200 and we are talking about spectacular seasons. Spahn's best ERA+ was 188 in 1953, when his actual ERA was 2.10. He topped 130 only twice. His career could be characterized as sustained excellence rather than otherworldly peak performance.

Bob Gibson was a force of nature in his prime. He won two Cy Young Awards and posted one of the best single seasons ever in 1968 when he went 22–9 with a ridiculous 1.12 ERA. That year, his ERA+ was an incredible 258. That year he also led the league in strikeouts with 268 and posted the league's best WHIP, which is a statistic that measures walks plus hits divided by innings pitched. His WHIP that year was a tremendous 0.853. To give some context, the league average WHIP that year was 1.201, so Gibson was in a class by himself in terms of keeping people off

---

[6] Ebbets Field was just 297 feet to right field and 399 to center, both very short distances for major-league ballparks.

base and, once they got there, from scoring. Moreover, he posted an amazing 13 shutouts, throwing 304.2 innings over the course of the season.

In 1969, his win-loss record was worse (just 16–13), but his ERA was still spectacular, at 2.18. For a dominant pitcher, he did not strike out as many batters as one might think. The most strikeouts per nine innings he ever had was 8.4 in 1970, which was indeed excellent, but again, not out of this world. During his seven-year peak from 1966 to 1972, he posted a 134–72 record with a 2.42 ERA, 145 ERA+, 1.078 WHIP, and 7.5 k/9 (strikeouts per nine innings pitched). All outstanding numbers, and he backed it up by being phenomenal in the postseason. In nine career World Series games, he went 7–2 with a 1.89 ERA, leading his Cardinals to two championships (one against the Yankees in 1964, and another against the Red Sox in 1967) and one seventh-game loss. Perhaps the best game he ever pitched was Game 1 of the 1968 World Series, as he beat the Tigers 4–0 by throwing nine innings of five-hit, one-walk shutout baseball, striking out 17. He beat Denny McLain in that game. All McLain did that season was go 31–6 with a 1.96 ERA en route to winning the AL Cy Young and MVP Awards. Gibson was an all-time great, but he still falls short of "greatest of all time" status.

What about Tom Seaver? Over the course of his career, Seaver won 311 games and posted an ERA of 2.86. His peak in particular was tremendous. From 1968 to 1975, he went 152–83 with a 2.45 ERA, 145 ERA+, 1.044 WHIP, and 7.9 k/9. He led the league in ERA three times, won three Cy Young Awards, and finished in the top ten in CYA balloting six times over this stretch. Four times he finished with an ERA of 2.25 or below. He led the league in k/9 six times, topping out at 9.1 in 1971, a year in which he also posted a 1.76 ERA. He was also a clutch postseason performer, winning the World Series with the Mets in 1969 and delivering a 2.77 ERA in eight career postseason starts.

Seaver belongs in the conversation for greatest of all time, but even he can't hold a candle to Sandy Koufax. Koufax' career was much shorter than Seaver's. Seaver pitched for twenty years; Koufax just twelve. As a result, Koufax won "only" 165 games. And his career took some time to get going, as it wasn't until his seventh season that he became a great pitcher. His breakout year was in 1961, when he went 18–13 with a 3.52 ERA. He would follow that up with a terrific 1962 season in which he posted a 2.54 ERA and won 15 games. He regularly struck out more than 10 batters over nine innings, but the early part of his career was troubled with wildness, as he regularly walked nearly four and a half batters per nine innings. His career took off once he figured out the element of control.

For Koufax, it's not his longevity or overall career that we are interested in here. We are asking the question about peak performance, and Koufax' peak was mind-bogglingly great. His last four seasons (he retired at the age of thirty) were as good as you'll ever see. From 1963 to 1966, he went 97–27 (.782) with a 1.86 ERA, 172 ERA+, 0.909 WHIP, and 9.3 k/9. He led the league in wins three of those four years, in ERA all four of those years (plus the year before just for fun), ERA+ twice, WHIP three times (and again, also the season before), and k/9 three times (six overall in his career). He also pitched 311 or more innings in three of the four seasons and threw a ridiculous 54 complete games over the last two seasons. His strikeout-to-walk ratio during this four-year stretch was 4.74, an absolutely spectacular number.

Long story short, there's nothing anyone can say that's negative about Koufax' four-year peak. It's difficult to imagine anyone being better. Hold on to Koufax, because we will come back to him, but at the moment, he's the clear leader in the clubhouse.

The last cluster of pitchers to look at would be classified as modern pitchers. In this group are Greg Maddux, Randy Johnson, Roger Clemens, Clayton Kershaw, Mariano Rivera, and Pedro Martínez.

Let's start with Rivera, not because he's a lesser pitcher, but because he falls in a different category altogether. In 2019, he was elected as the first ever unanimous first-ballot selection. That alone speaks to the immense respect that everyone associated with the sport has for him. He is the all-time saves leader. His career numbers are staggering: 1,115 games pitched, 652 saves, 221 ERA, 205 career ERA+. It's difficult to determine his "peak," because for Rivera, he was great his entire career. For example, consider this four-year stretch from 1996 to 1999: 21–10, 1.95 ERA, 129 saves, 242 ERA+, 1.027 WHIP, 8.3 k/9. Or this four-year stretch from 2003 to 2006: 21–13, 1.69 ERA, 170 saves, 261 ERA+, 0.978 WHIP, 7.9 k/9. Or this four-year stretch from ages thirty-eight to forty-one (2008–2011): 13–13, 1.71 ERA, 160 saves, 259 ERA+, 0.821 WHIP, 8.8 k/9.

It's hard to pinpoint exactly when Rivera was at his best, because he's simply always been phenomenal. As a forty-three-year-old in his final season (2013), he still saved 44 games, posted a 2.11 ERA, 190 ERA+, and 1.047 WHIP. He was never anything less than ridiculously great. We haven't even gotten to his postseason record yet. As the anchor of so many great Yankee teams, he pitched in an astounding 96 postseason games, and over 141.0 innings saved 42 games against just 5 blown saves, and posted an insane 0.70 ERA and 0.759 WHIP to go along with a solid 7.0 k/9. His cut fastball is one of the greatest pitches in all of baseball history.

There is nothing negative anyone has ever said, or could ever say, about Rivera the pitcher and, more importantly, Rivera the man. There is a reason why only one relief pitcher is on the list of greatest pitchers of all time, and there is a reason why it's Rivera. But therein lies the problem for his case. He was a relief pitcher. Yes, by far the greatest relief pitcher ever, but a reliever nonetheless. His 141 postseason innings were phenomenal, but Andy Pettitte, a very good pitcher for a long time but never in the "greatest of all time" discussion, pitched 276.2 postseason innings over the same time frame. Relievers simply cannot make the same impact in the game as starters. Great starters will throw seven innings compared with one or two by relievers. This dispropor- tionate usage is reflected in a stat called "wins above replacement" (WAR). It's complicated, but suffice it to say that one's WAR value is impacted by quality of performance but also amount of performance. One inning of A+ ball is not as valuable as eight innings of A ball. To illustrate this, let's compare two of Rivera's own seasons.

In 1996, he was not yet the "closer" for New York. John Wetteland had that job, and Rivera was the main setup guy in the Yankee bullpen. He went 8–3 and saved five games, with a 2.09 ERA, 240 ERA+, 0.994 WHIP, and 10.9 k/9. He was also worth 5.0 wins above replacement. In 2008, he went 6–5 and saved 39 games, with a 1.40 ERA, 316 ERA+, 0.665 WHIP, and 9.8 k/9. He was worth 4.3 wins above replacement. If a pitch- er's job is to prevent base runners and runs, how could Rivera be worth more wins in 1996 than he was in 2008, when his WHIP was 0.329 better, his ERA 0.69 better, and his ERA+ 76 better? The answer lies mainly in the number of innings pitched. Rivera threw 70.2 innings in 2008 (not a small number for a closer) but 107.0 in 1996. Those 30 extra innings were immensely valuable to the Yankees, and as a result, Rivera was worth more in 1996 than he was in 2008, even though he was a better pitcher in 2008.

It's this reality that rules Rivera out from the conversation of greatest pitcher of all time. He was unquestionably the greatest reliever of all time, and because of his greatness both in peak and over time, he deserves to be in this conversation, but he cannot be the greatest overall pitcher ever.

Let's look next at Randy Johnson. He pitched twenty-two years, the first five of which were fine, but nothing special. Then he became, at age twenty-nine, the Big Unit, going 19–8 with a 3.24 ERA and striking out 308 hitters. Over the course of his career, he won 303 games against just 166 losses and finished with a career ERA of 3.29 and a whopping 4,875 strikeouts (number two of all time behind Nolan Ryan's 5,714). He was a tremendous pitcher for a long, long time, specializing in strikeouts. Nine times he led the league in strikeouts and k/9. He also won five Cy Young Awards and finished in the top five in CYA voting an amazing nine times. And his peak…let's talk about *that*.

From 1999 to 2002, he was as dominant as a pitcher can be. He went 81–27 (.750) with a 2.48 ERA, 187 ERA+, 1.044 WHIP, and 12.4 k/9. He won four straight Cy Young Awards. Over that four-year stretch, he led the league in wins once, ERA three times, innings pitched twice, strikeouts four times, ERA+ four times, and k/9 four times. He also had a spectacular 4.92 k/ bb ratio, which means that not only was he striking out a ton of guys, he wasn't walking many either. Over those four seasons, he *averaged* 354 strikeouts a season.

It's difficult to conceive of a better four-year stretch than this. Comparing this four-year run to Koufax', we see that Johnson stacks up nicely against the Dodger lefty.

Koufax: 97–27 (.782) with a 1.86 ERA, 172 ERA+, 0.909 WHIP, and 9.3 k/9

Johnson: 81–27 (.750) with a 2.48 ERA, 187 ERA+, 1.044 WHIP, and 12.4 k/9

Koufax had the better winning percentage, ERA, and WHIP, but Johnson had the better ERA+ (in other words, he pitched in a much better time in baseball history for hitters) and strikeout numbers. It's hard to say which pitcher was better. Johnson was worth 38.1 wins above replacement during this stretch, while Koufax was worth 36.3. As great as Koufax was, Johnson may have been better at his peak. Call them co-leaders in the clubhouse.

Now we come to Greg Maddux. Like Johnson, Maddux pitched very well for a long period of time, amassing 355 career wins over a twenty-three-year career. For Maddux, we will look at his four-year peak and then his seven-year peak. His four-year peak is unquestionably from 1992 to 1995, when he, too, won four straight Cy Young Awards. During that time, he went 75–29 (.721), with a 1.98 ERA, 202 ERA+, 0.953 WHIP, and 7.0 k/9. He was a different kind of pitcher than Johnson. To illustrate how different the times were, Maddux was not considered a "strikeout pitcher," despite striking out seven batters every nine innings. But Gibson *was* considered a strikeout pitcher, and during his best stretch, he struck out 7.9 per 9 innings. Maddux won with impeccable control and masterful changes in speed. Johnson would blow hitters away with 99 mph heat, while Maddux would drop a soft, 73 mph changeup on the black that hitters could only roll gently to first base.

The following story encapsulates Greg Maddux. Ed Graney, in a 2014 article for the *Las Vegas Review-Journal*, tells a tale of an at-bat between Maddux and his nemesis, Luis Gonzalez of

Arizona. Gonzalez was one of the few players to have success against Maddux, hitting .325 with 10 homers in just 135 plate appearances against the ace pitcher. Graney writes, "It was during this time that Maddux spoke up in a certain pregame meeting: He told Cox that if Gonzalez came up with runners in scoring position and an open base, to go ahead and call for a walk. It happened. Arizona had runners at second and third with two outs late in the game when Cox told Mazzone to go talk with Maddux and confirm the plan. 'I go out and say, "Here's the guy you wanted to walk," Mazzone said. "Greg says, 'Give me two pitches. If I fall behind 2–0, I'll walk him. But I think I can pop him up to third in foul territory on the second pitch.' Well, he throws a cutter above the hands on the second pitch, and Luis pops up to third in foul territory for the third out."

Maddux had the ability to control the strike zone, to change speeds, to induce weak contact, like no pitcher ever had. His fastball averaged less than 85 miles an hour, but he dominated as if he threw 105. We can compare his four-year peak with Koufax and Johnson:

Koufax: 97–27 (.782) with a 1.86 ERA, 172 ERA+, 0.909 WHIP, and 9.3 k/9

Johnson: 81–27 (.750) with a 2.48 ERA, 187 ERA+, 1.044 WHIP, and 12.4 k/9

Maddux: 75–29 (.721), with a 1.98 ERA, 202 ERA+, 0.953 WHIP, and 7.0 k/9

But Maddux' peak extended longer than that. He added three more years onto that stretch, which weren't quite as good but which were still phenomenal in their own right. Over the next three seasons, he would go 52–24 with a 2.38 ERA, 178 ERA+, and 0.987 WHIP, finishing in the top five in Cy Young voting all three seasons. So his seven-year true peak was just absurd: 127–53 (.706), 2.15 ERA, 190 ERA+, 0.968 WHIP, 6.9 k/9, four Cy Young Awards, and seven straight top five finishes in CYA voting; something never done by any other pitcher in history.

Maddux' four-year peak may (or may not) be equivalent to Koufax and Johnson, but the fact that it extended to seven seasons puts him past the other two.

What about Roger Clemens? Part of the challenge with Clemens' career is that his "peak" was scattered throughout his career. He had spectacular seasons in 1986, 1990, 1997, 1998, 2004, and 2005. But mixed in there were some years that weren't quite so good. For example, in 1993, he went 11–14 with a 4.46 ERA. In 1995 he went 10–5 with a 4.18 ERA. In 1999, he went 14–10 with a 4.60 ERA. In 2002, he went 13–6 with a 4.35 ERA. So pinpointing a true peak for Clemens is challenging.

There is no doubt, of course, that his overall career is one of the best ever. He won a record seven Cy Young Awards and finished with 354 wins and the third most strikeouts in history, with 4,672. He also struck out 20 hitters in a game twice, showing that when he was on, he was utterly dominant. From a statistical standpoint, his peak may be the three-year period from 1990 to 1992, when he went 57–27 (.679), with a 2.34 ERA, 180 ERA+, 1.067 WHIP, and 7.9 k/9. But that was followed by two out of three seasons with an ERA of 4.18 or higher.

Moreover, there's the elephant in the room with Clemens. He was named in the 2007 Mitchell Report, which documented illegal steroid use in the sport. His former trainer, Brian McNamee, testified that he had repeatedly injected Clemens with Winstrol, an anabolic steroid. Clemens denied the claim, but Hall of Fame voters have not given him the benefit of the doubt. So the man with the most Cy Young Awards in history, a twenty-four-year career ERA of 3.12, a phenomenal ERA+ of 143, and a WHIP of 1.17 still is not enshrined in Cooperstown.

Clemens' overall career may have been one of the best ever, but these challenges take him out of the "greatest of all time" running, because we are talking about peak performance, and his peak was too scattered, littered with subpar seasons and controversy over steroid use.

That brings us to Clayton Kershaw. The only active pitcher in the entire group, Kershaw's career has been nothing less than spectacular. But the numbers…good lord, the numbers are hard to fathom in today's day and age. He has had a true seven-year peak, from 2011 to 2017, during which time he went 118–41 (.742), with a 2.10 ERA, 179 ERA+, 0.913 WHIP, and 10.1 k/9. Over that stretch, he won three Cy Young Awards and finished in the top five all seven years. In those seven seasons, he led the league in wins three times, ERA five times, strikeouts three times, ERA+ four times, WHIP four times, and k/9 twice. The last four of those seasons, his strikeout-to-walk ratio was a preposterous 8.02.

Kershaw is already a lock for the Hall of Fame, and he's just thirty-three years of age. From the age of twenty-one on, even as his stuff has diminished in recent years, he's been nothing less than a great pitcher. Even his 2019 campaign, which would be considered a "down" year for him, he went 16–5 with a 3.03 ERA, 1.043 WHIP, and 9.5 k/9.[7] He deserves to be in this conversation, even at his young age, and the fact that he's

---

[7] In the COVID-shortened 2020 season, Kershaw returned to dominance, going 6–2 with a 2.16 ERA, 0.84 WHIP, and 9.6 K/9. Moreover, he finally won his first World Series, winning two games against the Tampa Bay Rays, giving up just seven hits, three walks, and three runs in 11.2 innings, while striking out 14.

a current player with perhaps several more seasons still in the tank helps support that.

But is his peak as good as Pedro Martínez? We began this conversation because we were considering Pedro's place in history. As spectacular as Koufax', Johnson's, Maddux', and Kershaw's peaks were, nothing compares to the seven-year run Martínez had from 1997 to 2003. Never before has the sport seen the kind of dominance Pedro delivered over that seven-year peak stretch.

First, let's just consider the fact that he won three Cy Young Awards, finished second twice, and third once. The year he didn't finish near the top was in 2001, when he got hurt and only pitched in 18 games. But even then he posted a 2.39 ERA and struck out 12.6 batters per nine innings. Before the injury, Pedro was on track to win the CYA again. He finished in the top 22 of MVP voting those same six seasons.

Now let's look at some of the numbers. Over this seven-year stretch, he went 118–36 (.766), with a 2.20 ERA, 213 ERA+, 0.940 WHIP, and 11.3 k/9. Moreover, his k/bb ratio was an astounding 5.59. Every one of those stats is absurdly good. But what must be considered is the context in which he pitched.

The so-called "steroids era" began following the 1994–1995 strike that wiped out the last 50 games of the 1994 season and the playoffs as well. Baseball had no World Series champion that year, and fan interest waned following the strike. Baseball needed some "juice," as it were, and numerous players began using steroids. 1998 featured the amazing home run battle between Mark McGwire and Sammy Sosa. McGwire hit 70 homers that year, and Sosa would hit 60+ three times. Barry Bonds joined the fun and proceeded to put up offensive numbers that were incomprehensible. He hit 73 home runs in 2001 and had OPS numbers above 1.275 for four straight seasons.

In 1992, teams averaged 4.12 runs per game. That rose steadily, and from 1994 to 2001, teams averaged 4.92 runs per game. In 1999 and 2000, teams scored 5.08 and 5.16 runs per game, respectively. When Gibson was dominant in 1968, teams averaged 3.42 runs per game. When Seaver pitched in the early '70s, teams scored in the high threes per game. In 1990, when Clemens won his third Cy Young Award, teams averaged 4.26 runs per game.

We think of the modern game as being full of offense, and to be sure, it is. Clayton Kershaw has put up incredible numbers in a home run–happy era. And in 2019, baseball posted its highest-scoring season since 2006. But during Kershaw's seven-year peak from 2011 to 2017, teams averaged 4.32 runs per game. During Pedro's seven-year peak from 1997 to 2003, teams averaged 4.84 runs per game. That's better than half-a-run difference per game. In Maddux' seven-year stretch from 1992 to 1998, teams averaged 4.73 runs per game. Moreover, consider the OPS numbers teams put up during their respective seven-year stretches. Maddux: .747, Martínez: .762, Kershaw: .724. Since the dead ball era was over, Pedro Martínez pitched in the heart of the greatest offensive stretch the sport has ever seen.

And he put up mind-boggling numbers smack in the middle of that.

The key number in support of Pedro's greatness is 213. That's his ERA+ over his seven-year peak period. Over those seven seasons, he posted *five* ERA+ numbers of 202 or greater. Kershaw's best ever was 197. Maddux reached 200 twice, and his best ERA+ numbers were 271 (1994) and 260 (1995). Randy Johnson never reached 200. Clemens did it three times, in 1990 (211), 1997 (222), and 2005 (226). Seaver never got to 200. Neither did Koufax. Gibson did it once, during his ridiculous

1968 season (258). Of the old-timers, Cy Young did it once. Keefe did it once in his first season when he pitched in just 12 games (105 innings). Grover Cleveland Alexander did it once. Walter Johnson did it four times, his best being 259 in 1913 (when his ERA was 1.14). Mathewson did it twice.

You get the point. Given the historical context in which he pitched, nobody dominated like Pedro did. He did it with pinpoint control. He did it with a blazing fastball in the high nineties. He did it with one of the best curveballs ever. He did it with intelligence and determination. He struck out guys at an amazing rate and hardly walked anyone. And he simply did not let you score.

His two-year über-peak was, relative to the era in which he played, the greatest two-year peak in baseball history. In 1999, he went 23–4 with a 2.07 ERA, 243 ERA+, 0.923 WHIP, 13.2 k/9, and 8.46 k/bb ratio. He was worth 9.8 wins above replacement. It is difficult to imagine performing better than that, but he did, in 2000, going 18–6 with a 1.74 ERA, 291 ERA+, 0.737 WHIP, 11.8 k/9, and 8.88 k/bb ratio. He was worth an astounding 11.7 wins above replacement. Mike Trout, who may go down as one of the five greatest players ever to play the game, has never had a WAR higher than 10.1.[8]

FiveThirtyEight.com, a website the focuses on statistical analysis of sports, economics, and politics, posted an article in 2016 talking about Martínez' greatness and compared him mainly to Maddux, Johnson, and Clemens. They have a metric that isn't easy to explain, but it's called a "pitcher score," and it incorporates significant amounts of pitching data to produce a number that means nothing except to provide a means of making a relative comparison between respective pitchers' performances. It may

---

[8] Through 2020.

seem like circular logic, but to sum up, the greater the score, the better the pitching performance. Pedro's dominance is illustrated by the number of top 100 peak games by each pitcher, by pitcher score rating.

Pedro: 55

Johnson: 25

Maddux: 18

Clemens: 2

Of the top 28 seasons by pitcher score, Pedro Martínez owns the top three of all time (2000, 2001, 1999). His 2002 season is #6. His 2003 season is #17. His 1998 season is #24, and his 1997 season is #28. So Pedro owns 7 of the top 28 seasons *ever* in terms of pitcher score. Maddux has three. Clemens has two. Johnson has seven as well but none in the top four. Koufax has one. This is all a long way of pointing out that when Pedro was at his best, there simply has never been anyone better. Period.

Four games in particular illustrate the greatness of Pedro Martínez. The first one came on June 3, 1995. He was still with the Expos, and they were facing the San Diego Padres. In a tense, scoreless game, Pedro threw nine perfect innings, striking out nine. The game went into extra innings, and he finally gave up a hit to the leadoff hitter. He ended up with the victory, giving up just the one hit in the tenth, but he did not get credit for a perfect game, because it extended into extra innings. Joey Hamilton, his opponent that day, was also brilliant, giving up just three hits and two walks over nine innings, keeping the Expos off the board.

The second game was on September 10, 1999. He was facing the New York Yankees, who were in the midst of their great late '90s dynasty, during which they won four championships in five seasons. In the heat of the pennant race, in raucous Yankee

Stadium, Martínez went the full nine innings, allowing only one hit and one run—a solo homer by Chili Davis in the second inning—walking nobody and striking out 17. He struck out eight of the last nine Yankee batters in one of the most dominant performances ever seen on a baseball diamond, given the setting and caliber of opponent.

In the playoffs in 1999, he had two legendary performances. The first tells us all we need to know about Martínez. In Game 1 of the divisional round against Cleveland, Pedro had to leave the game due to a back injury. Boston fell behind two games to none before rallying to win the next two and send the series back to Cleveland for the final Game 5. Cleveland battered Boston pitching through the first three innings and held an 8–5 lead going into the fourth. Boston scored one to make it 8–6, and at that point, Martínez entered the game, to the astonishment of basically…everybody. He couldn't throw harder than 90 mph (he was clocked at 99 mph during the all-star game earlier in the year, when he struck out five of the first six National League hitters), and at any moment, his back could seize up on him.

Pedro would go on to pitch six straight shutout innings, no-hitting the Indians (who had hit three homers in three innings already) and striking out eight to give the Sox a chance to come back. They did, and won the game 12–8. Troy O'Leary was the hitting star, with two homers and seven RBIs, but it was Pedro who won the game for Boston.

During his induction to the Red Sox Hall of Fame, he reminisced about this performance. "It was the playoffs, it was everything on the line, including my career, because a lot of people see the game, yes, yes, yes, yes, it was a great game. But I put my career in jeopardy. And a lot of people don't realize how bad I was [injured]. And the next game, even the next game that I pitched here, I know that it went by because we had a great game and we ended up beating the Yankees and all that. But it was after that [Game 5] that every shoulder problem I had developed."

In the next series against New York, the Yankees were up two games to none, and Martínez faced off against Roger Clemens. He won 13–1 and dominated New York, throwing seven scoreless innings, allowing two hits and two walks, while striking out 12, his back still a mess.

At his best, Pedro Martínez was the single greatest pitcher the sport has ever seen. But by 2004, he was past his peak. When he faced the heart of the Yankee lineup in the fifth inning of Game 5, he was no longer the great *Pedro Martínez*. He was merely a very good pitcher. He was good enough to get New York's top three hitters in order on 16 pitches—Rodriguez walked, Sheffield grounded into a double play, and Matsui lined out—and Boston came up in the bottom of the inning, still holding a 2–1 lead. During the Matsui at-bat, Martínez buzzed him with a fastball high and inside that shook Matsui. Before this at-bat, he had been 12–22 in the series. From this moment on, he would go just 2–12 the rest of the way.

"We had to do it," Martínez would say afterward. "He was leaning and hitting everything out over the plate. He was feeling too comfortable. He needed to go back and I made a statement. 'I'm going to pitch you inside, and you need to move back,' so that I could get back to what I need to do. So I just busted him in and busted him again and busted him again. Then the next day, everybody that saw what I did went on to do the same thing, so I cooled him off. We cooled him off that day."

MUSSINA, FOR HIS part, kept mowing Boston hitters down. He was never in Pedro's class, but he was a pro's pro and had many quality seasons in his own right. He was elected into the Hall of Fame in 2019, and he sure knew how to pitch. Knowing he couldn't allow the Red Sox to expand their lead, he surrendered a single to Cabrera and then got the heart of Boston's own potent lineup—Ortiz, Ramirez, and Millar—on just nine pitches. He was keeping the Yankees in the game.

After five, Boston led by one. The game was just about to get very interesting.

6

THE SIXTH INNING

The Yankees won 101 games in 2004. They not only had a fearsome top four in the lineup, but they had quality hitters behind them. They finished second in the AL in runs scored (Boston was number one), first in home runs, second in OPS (Boston was number one), and first in OPS+. After Matsui, the Yankees were to bring up Bernie Williams (22 HR, 108 OPS+), Jorge Posada (21 HR, 131 OPS+), and Rubén Sierra (17 HR in just 307 at-bats). Trouble lurked around every corner.

Pedro was at 82 pitches at the start of the sixth. Francona was hoping to get one more inning out of him, and maybe, if everything broke right, two, before turning it over to his bullpen. The problem, of course, was that his bullpen was on fumes from the long game the previous night. And not just that, but from Game 3 as well. Over the course of the two games, Red Sox' relievers were forced to throw a lot of pitches:

Mendoza: 20 in Game 3
Leskanic: 15 in Game 3, 13 in Game 4
Wakefield: 64 in Game 3
Embree: 14 in Game 3, 30 in Game 4
Myers: 42 in Game 3, 4 in Game 4
Timlin: 37 in Game 4
Foulke: 50 in Game 4

Francona knew he would need to get some outs from these guys, but he also knew that should they make it to Game 6, Curt Schilling was the scheduled starter. Schilling, however, was a gigantic *if*, given the injury to his ankle. He would start, but he might only be able to go a couple of innings before the ankle gave out, and Boston might need to get 20 or more outs from the pen. That game would be played the next night, so there wasn't even time to rest. He needed more innings out of Martínez.

At the start of the inning, Joe Buck said, "The Red Sox need Pedro Martínez to have a quick and easy inning. It's been a battle every frame. He has not retired the Yankees in order yet tonight, with that race against the pitch count."

On a 1–1 pitch, Williams lofted a ball to shallow left. Manny Ramirez, never known for his fielding, raced in and made a nice catch. Three-pitch outs were just what the doctor ordered for Pedro and the Red Sox.

Posada was next. In the bottom of the fifth, Ramirez had fouled a pitch straight back and off Posada's right hand. Catchers typically keep that hand protected, but the ball caught his hand flush. Tending to Posada meant a several minute game delay. They determined that he was okay to continue, but it was not clear how much it would affect Posada's grip on the bat.

On the first pitch, a sinking curveball, Posada chopped a high bouncer over Martínez' head into no-man's land between second and short. Posada, never a fast runner, was still able to beat it out easily, without even a throw. A clunky infield hit put a runner on first, with Sierra coming up.

Leiter commented, "You can execute a quality pitch to exploit a hitter's weakness...after that you have no idea where the ball will end, how it will end, who fields it...no control."

Martínez started off with a wicked changeup that Sierra flailed at helplessly for strike one. Pedro threw the same pitch again, but this time Sierra hit a soft line drive to left center that advanced Posada to second. Suddenly the Yankees were in business with two on and one out. Still, McCarver chided Posada for not being more aggressive. "Oh, that was the time to go to third base. That's cautious base running by Posada. Regardless of who fields the ball, you've gotta be on third base with one out. Ball hit off the end of the bat, it wasn't hit hard. Posada is not one of the better base runners in the American League. If Ramirez fields the ball, he's got a tougher throw, and if Damon fields the ball, he's got a poor arm. So regardless of who fields the ball, you've got to be on third." In the dugout, Yankee players had been screaming for Posada to keep going. To McCarver's point, there was a huge difference between being on third and remaining at second with one out, as New York needed a hit to score Posada from second, but if he was on third, a ground ball or fly ball to the outfield could have done the trick. Either way, Pedro was in a jam.

Clark stepped in, with a chance to tie the game or give New York the lead with an extra-base hit. He hit 28 combined extra-base hits in 2004 in just 253 at-bats, but his career-best season would come in 2005 with Arizona (.304, 30 home runs, 87 RBIs, 154 OPS+). His average in 2004 was just .221, but he was more than capable of delivering a big hit. Ironically, he could do serious damage to his former club, for whom he played so poorly in 2002.

Pedro started him off with an 88 mph sinking fastball that was low for ball one. A "Let's go Red Sox!" chant filled the stands. Clark fouled the next pitch—an 89 mph fastball, this one low and away—off into the left field stands for strike one.

Dave O'Brien commented, "Clark, a big man with good power. Pedro, a smaller, more slender figure on that hill, and occasionally, he can still rear back and grab a 96, 97 mile an hour fastball. A few years ago that was routine for Martínez. It is no longer the case. But every so often, when he needs it most, he can get it."

A Martínez slider on the outside corner made the count 1–2. Martínez, looking for the strikeout, then threw his hardest pitch of the game, a 94 mph fastball, inside for ball two. That pitch may have taken extra effort, as he had been throwing in the upper 80s for the last two innings. Another fastball—this one at 93—missed low, and Clark did a good job laying off. The count was full.

Martínez hung a change, and Clark lifted a fly ball fairly deep down the right field line, but it hooked foul to keep the count at 3–2. Sutcliffe commented, "Look at the location. He is very, very lucky that was not a home run, a lot like what John Olerud did in his last start in this very same inning [a sixth-inning home run off Pedro in Game 2 in Yankee Stadium]. You gotta get smarter. You have to tell yourself, 'Hey, I don't have that great velocity. I have to get better with my command.' Think out over the plate, think down, get a ground ball."

Martínez was up to 94 pitches and was working hard to retire New York's number eight hitter. The crowd noise rising, Pedro threw a cut fastball low and away that Clark took. He took a step toward first base, thinking it was a ball, but Kellogg raised his hand and called it a strike. As if on cue from Sutcliffe, it was a great pitch with perfect location, and Pedro was just one out away from escaping the jam. "He just did it," Sutcliffe said. "What a big, big pitch, in a huge situation there. Painting that outside corner, he took a little bit off so that he could get it exactly where he wanted it."

"Nasty," said Leiter.

"Trouble for Pedro has been after 100 pitches," O'Brien said. "So he's five away from that, trying to get out of this inning."

But he wasn't out of the inning yet. Miguel Cairo, the number nine hitter, was next. Pedro started him off with a big curve that missed inside for ball one. On the second pitch, he fired a fastball inside that deflected off Cairo's triceps, then Varitek's face mask off the ricochet. Cairo was awarded first base, moving Sierra to second and Posada to third.

Up strode Derek Jeter, prompting Buck to say, "This is the biggest at-bat of the night." Jeter had been having a rough night to this point, going 0–3 with two strikeouts. Over the course of his career, Jeter would hit .363 with a .418 on-base percentage and a .943 OPS against starting pitchers when facing them for the fourth time. Those numbers dropped to just .272 with a .362 on-base percentage and a .737 OPS when facing a reliever for the first time in a game. From a tactical standpoint, this would have been a good time to bring in a reliever, but it was still just the sixth, and Francona needed more out of Martínez. He was in a bind.

Jeter was also a good hitter with two outs and the bases loaded over the course of his career, hitting .321 with a .407 on-base percentage in such situations. He was a tough out in big spots. He was also a hitter who willingly put the ball into all fields, which made him difficult to pitch to. If you threw inside on him, he'd pull it. If you pitched him outside, he'd take it to right field. He had over the course of his career nearly as many hits to right field as he did to left.

When general manager Dan Duquette traded for Pedro Martínez following the 1997 season, he said, "This is a huge acquisition for us. When you have a number one pitcher, that makes you that much better. This past season, the Red Sox lacked an ace pitcher. This is the kind of trade that when you go to bed as a general manager, you dream of."

One hitter Martínez got out with great frequency was none other than Derek Jeter. During Martínez' Red Sox career, Jeter hit just .247 off him and was Pedro's second-biggest strikeout victim, behind Jorge Posada. It was two innings sooner than the previous year, but Francona was facing the same exact decision Grady Little had the year before. A tiring Pedro, with runners on base, and Boston clinging to a small lead, in a must-win game. Like Little, Francona elected to stick with Martínez.

As Jeter dug in, Buck said, "For the Yankees, they have one of the most clutch postseason performers in franchise history at the plate, Derek Jeter."

"We talked about how this is the time of the year for heroes," said Sutcliffe. "This man has already made his mark. He knows all about October."

Joe Castiglione drew listeners' attention to the escalating pitch count. "He's almost at a hundred pitches," Castiglione said. "Ninety-seven. You wonder if this might be it, because he's really had to pitch with a lot of pressure all day."

The first pitch was a 91 mph fastball well outside that Jeter easily let go by for ball one. Pedro stared in as the crowd looked on anxiously. There was a buzz, but it was a typical Boston "oh crap, here come the Yankees" buzz. Everyone in the park was a bundle of nerves. Pedro reared back and blew a letter-high 90 mph fastball past Jeter, who took a solid rip but missed. The count was 1–1.

"That was his ninety-ninth pitch," said O'Brien. "And the trouble mark for Pedro seems to be right around a hundred pitches."

The fateful pitch. Pedro stared in, chomping on his gum. Jeter dug in and waved his bat, ready for the delivery. Martínez threw a cut fastball on the outer half of the plate and Jeter hit a low line drive down the right field line, fair by a few feet. It rolled into the corner. Trot Nixon raced over to field it. It took a funny hop that encouraged Cairo to try to score all the way from first. Nixon fired a throw to Varitek, who caught the ball in front of the plate. Cairo dove around the lunging tag, sneaking his arm under Varitek's glove. He was safe. Jeter wound up with a three-run double, advancing to third on the throw, and vaulting the Yankees into a 4–2 lead. Jeter pumped his fist as Sierra and Cairo hugged behind home plate.

"A tremendous slide around the tag by Cairo!" O'Brien cried.

"Just add another chapter to the book on Derek Jeter," said Sutcliffe. "And his tremendous job in the postseason…He went right down the line on the pitch on the outer half, and now they're off to the races…Derek Jeter, it's his time of the year."

Pedro was over 100 pitches and still not out of the woods. Alex Rodriguez was up next, and Martínez was losing it quickly. Still, Francona let him pitch.

Ball one came on a curve that missed badly outside, prompting a mound visit by pitching coach Dave Wallace.

"He's done," Sutcliffe said. "History has proven that I don't know how many times. They keep asking for more and more out of Pedro Martínez. He's not the guy that he was four years ago."

The bullpen finally began to stir in right field.

Martínez drilled Rodriguez with the next pitch, and suddenly, New York had runners at the corners with Sheffield coming up.

"If that's not a sign that Pedro is done, I don't know what is," said an exasperated O'Brien. "The Red Sox in the dugout suddenly look completely lost."

Pedro remained in the game. His first pitch to Sheffield missed low for ball one. The Yankees could smell blood.

Mike Timlin and Mike Myers were warming for Boston. "This should have been happening ten minutes ago," mused O'Brien.

Pedro's second pitch, another curve, missed badly outside for ball two. He snapped a curve in there for the first strike of the at-bat. A fastball low made it 3–1. Very dangerous territory for Martínez with the fearsome Sheffield eager to deliver the killer blow.

O'Brien said, "Three and one, as the pitch count rises, up to a hundred and six. He's moments away from having to face the hottest hitter on the planet right now, Hideki Matsui."

Sutcliffe replied, "He can't let him face him! I dunno…we'll see." Sutcliffe had been calling for Myers to have already been warmed and ready to face the imposing lefty. Myers was what was known as a LOOGY—a "Lefty One Out GuY." As bullpens had transformed over the years, every team employed a specialist like this, a guy designed to come into the game in the late innings to get that tough left-handed hitter out.[9] Often, they threw from a wicked sidearm angle. Myers was one of those guys, and he was very good at his job. In 2004, Myers allowed right-handed hitters to bat .328 with a .968 OPS against him; but lefties only managed

---

[9] A new rule change for the 2020 season required relievers to face a minimum of three hitters or pitch till the end of the inning. This change has meant that the days of the LOOGY may be over, as pitchers need to be able to handle multiple batters, hitting from both sides of the plate.

to hit .240 with a .683 OPS against the sidewinding left-handed specialist. Hitters like Hideki Matsui, in big spots, were exactly the reason Myers was on the team.

Buck commented, "With Matsui on deck and Myers up in the bullpen, this could be it for Pedro Martínez." McCarver replied, "I would think so."

Martínez missed badly with a change to walk Sheffield, and the Fenway faithful were, almost to a person, wondering when Pedro was coming out. Both FOX and MLB broadcast crews were sure that it would be here, as Matsui strode to the plate with the bases loaded and a chance to break the game wide open, and end the Red Sox' season in the process. Myers was ready. Matsui—a much more effective hitter against right-handed pitchers than against lefties (he hit .314 with a .977 OPS against righties in 2004 versus .265 with a .776 OPS against lefties)—walked toward the box. Everyone anticipated Francona coming out of the dugout to make the change. This was Grady Little all over again.

O'Brien: "He missed badly there for ball four and the bases are loaded again for the Yankees. Have we now seen the last of Pedro Martínez?" The question hung in the air. Dave Wallace was on the phone. He threw up his hands in exasperation. The crowd anticipated a move right here. A smart baseball fan base, they knew that Myers vs. Matsui was the proper call.

Francona stayed put. It was almost incomprehensible that Red Sox fans were witnessing a virtual repeat of history from the year before. In an article for BosSports.net from January 2004, Bob George wrote about the Little fiasco and the new manager, Terry Francona. "Francona and his stats can fail just as easily as Little did. But Francona won't likely fail in the same, tragic way Little did."

Yet here he was, doing just that. Pedro's pitch count rising too high. Dozens of incredibly high-stress, high-leverage pitches. The season on the line. Yankee hitters fighting off tough pitches and hitting the ball where Red Sox fielders weren't. Walks. Hit batsmen. The inning—and season—falling apart. The Red Sox manager stubbornly sticking with Martínez when all signs evident to everyone else in the world showed it was long past time to remove him. Rome burning while Nero fiddles.

O'Brien couldn't believe it. "Matsui's getting in! He's gonna face Martínez! This is a major roll of the dice by the Red Sox manager."

Pedro still had one out to get. Did the legendary pitcher have it in him to get the job done?

His first pitch to Matsui was a slider that missed inside for ball one. A change missed outside for ball two, putting Matsui in the spot every hitter wants to be in.

"It's just remarkable to see a Red Sox manager make the same mistake in a crucial spot against the Yankees in the ALCS in back-to-back Octobers," O'Brien said.

Martínez buried a strike on a cut fastball that Matsui let go by. At 2–0, a hitter is looking for his pitch to drive, and obviously what Martínez threw wasn't what Matsui was looking for. The count was 2–1.

"You wonder what Matsui was looking for," said McCarver. "He gets a 2–0 cookie down the pipe and takes it."

Martínez delivered a sinking change that Matsui roped to right. Nixon charged in and lunged for it, snaring it. He rolled to the ground and secured the ball for the third out of the inning. Pedro exhaled as he walked off the mound, having given up three runs and the lead, but also having kept Boston in the game. Down two runs with four turns at bat left, the Sox were still in it.

Mike Mussina was dealing. From the second through the fifth innings, he faced 15 Red Sox hitters. Two got singles, one reached on Jeter's error, and the rest were retired, six by strikeout. He had settled in nicely after the rough first.

Nixon led off the sixth—it is strange how often it seems that a player making a wonderful play to end the previous half inning comes up to lead off the next inning and worked the count full. "The Red Sox offense really hasn't figured out Mussina to this point," said Buck.

On the next pitch, Nixon hit a bullet to center. Williams sprinted in, slid, and made a superb backhand catch to rob him of a hit.

Varitek stepped in next, and Mussina threw a ball followed by a strike. Leiter pointed out that Mussina had gotten ahead of 16 straight batters. "You're gonna get an awful lot of guys out if you're constantly ahead 0–2, 1–2," he said. And on cue, Mussina dropped a sharp curve in for a strike to make the count 1–2. He missed to make it 2–2 as Varitek wouldn't chase, and then Varitek spoiled four straight pitches, fouling off a variety of Mussina offerings. On the ninth pitch of the at-bat, he grounded to third, and the sure-handed Rodriguez scooped it up and easily threw him out. Two down.

Mueller was up next and popped weakly to left to retire the side. The Yankees began the inning down 2–1 with a 36 percent chance of winning the game and ended the inning up 4–2 with an 80 percent chance of winning.

7

THE SEVENTH INNING

The previous night, Mike Timlin had relieved starter Derek Lowe in the top of the sixth, trying to protect a one-run lead. Over the next two innings, Timlin faced eight Yankee hitters and, after throwing 37 grueling pitches, left the game with the Red Sox down by one. With that rough Game 4 performance fresh in his mind, Timlin went to work in the seventh inning of Game 5 in relief of Martínez.

"Have we seen Pedro Martínez for the last time in a Red Sox uniform?" asked Trupiano on the radio broadcast.

Timlin got Bernie Williams to fly out to right and Posada to fly to left. Rubén Sierra was next, and on the first pitch he saw, he hit a high bounding grounder to Cabrera at short. Cabrera gunned to first, but Sierra, hustling all the way, barely beat it out for an infield hit. It was Sierra's fourth straight time on base (three hits plus a walk). He was having a big night for New York.

"Joe West deked the crowd," Trupiano said. "He started to go up with the out sign and then stretched the arms out to indicate 'safe.' But he got it right."

The Yankees, who exhibited terrific patience against Pedro, were swinging early in the count against Timlin. There was a reason for that. In Timlin's long career, opponents batted .315 against him on the first pitch, .344 against him on 2–0, .300 when the count was 1–1, and .355 when it was 2–1. But as the count deepened, hitters struggled. On a 1–2 count, batters hit just .170, and it wasn't much better when it was 2–2 (.195) or a full count (.211). The best way to get to Timlin was swinging early in the count, because he was typically around the plate.

Timlin had always been a classic ground ball pitcher. For the first thirteen years of his career, he had a ground ball to fly ball ratio of 1.25, indicating that his hard, sinking fastball was a problem for hitters to lift. But in 2004, the number had reversed, to 0.95, meaning that hitters now began to lift the ball more than hit it on the ground. That number would continue to head in that direction, over his last four seasons, as his ground ball to fly ball ratio dropped to 0.72, meaning he had become a major fly ball pitcher.

Still, it was fairly common for him to get hitters to put the ball on the ground. In his last two appearances in the ALCS, he had given up three infield hits. He was doing his job but not getting the results. A sturdy workhorse, he was a generally reliable reliever his whole career, pitching for Toronto, Seattle, Baltimore, and St. Louis before coming to Boston in 2003. Early in his career, he did good work for the Blue Jays in their two championship runs (1992, 1993), pitching to a 2.45 ERA in seven games. In 2003 with the Red Sox, he was lights out in the playoffs. He pitched in eight games in that playoff run alone (Boston played 12 games overall), allowing just one hit and two walks in 9.2 innings. He gave up zero runs throughout those playoffs.

The 2004 playoffs, however, were a different story. In six games up till Game 5 of the ALCS, he had allowed 10 hits, four walks, and six earned runs in just 5.1 innings, sporting a horrific 10.13 ERA. Opponents were hitting a tidy .400 with a 1.043 OPS against him. His 2004 playoff experience to this point had been a gigantic struggle, but he was a key member of the bullpen, and one of the most trusted arms Francona had available. An avid hunter, Timlin was also famous for his animal eye stew. Timlin once told Francona that his secret was "to use the whole eye. Ball and all."

Clark, who was 0–3 with two strikeouts, was next. Timlin threw over to first to check on Sierra. Clark beat the first pitch into the ground, a routine chopper to second. Bellhorn fielded it easily and underhanded to first to get the force out, and the side was retired. Timlin had done his job, needing just six pitches to record three outs.

IN THE BOTTOM of the inning, Mussina, who had thrown 103 pitches, came back out. He would be on a short leash, but he had been pitching so effectively, Joe Torre thought he might get him through the seventh, making the task for his bullpen, which had also worked a lot the previous night, easier.

Bellhorn led off. He was 0–2 and was having a miserable series, but he had hit the ball hard twice so far. He was clearly seeing the ball better, and that had to be an encouraging sign for him. Mussina pumped a fastball in for a strike, over the inside corner at the knees. On the second pitch, Bellhorn yanked the ball down the first base line, fair, and into the corner. Sheffield played the carom, but it took a funky hop away from him. Bellhorn hesitated rounding first, thinking he only could manage a single, but when he saw the ball get away from Sheffield, who slipped trying to retrieve it, he raced for second and made it easily.

Torre immediately came out to remove Mussina, who once again performed well for the Yankees in a big spot, and summoned 6'5" right-hander Tanyon Sturtze.

Sturtze was good enough to survive twelve years in the majors, but he never was a particularly effective pitcher at the big league level. His best season was in 2001 with Tampa Bay, when he pitched 195.1 innings to a 4.42 ERA. In 2004, he put up a 5.47 ERA and a 1.40 WHIP for New York. Runners got on base a lot against Sturtze, and many of them rounded the bases and made it home. On August 31, he came in to pitch in a disastrous 22–0 loss to Cleveland; and in three innings, he allowed six hits and seven runs. Two appearances later, he pitched in another Yankee disaster, a 17–8 loss to Kansas City. In two-thirds of an inning, he allowed five hits and seven runs.

But he had been pitching better at the end of the year. His last six appearances of the regular season, he pitched 12 innings, allowing just three hits, four walks, and no runs, while striking out 14 batters. Maybe he had found something. But playoff Sturtze had reverted to form, and over his first four appearances of the postseason, he had allowed six hits, three walks, and three runs over just five innings. The previous night, he had his best outing of the playoffs, pitching two shutout innings and throwing 25 pitches in the effort.

Torre, like Francona, didn't have many great options at this point in the game. Out came Worcester, Massachusetts native Sturtze to face Johnny Damon. His first pitch missed badly, as did his second. On the 2–0 pitch—a hitter's count—Damon hit a towering pop-up on the infield. Jeter strode over and corralled it for the first out of the inning. Damon's slump continued, and an unproductive out left Bellhorn at second.

Cabrera was next, and he and Sturtze engaged in a war. Sturtze started him off with a slider that Cabrera swung at and missed for strike one. He shook Posada off three times and then called time so the two of them could get on the same page. He threw a 91 mph fastball at the letters that Cabrera fought off for strike two. Just as Joe Buck commented on his good splitter, he threw one that missed way too low for Cabrera to be tempted to swing at. Ball one.

Another splitter down low, and this time Cabrera yanked it foul into the third base stands. The fifth pitch was his best fastball, a 94 mph, letter high delivery, and Cabrera fouled it back to stay alive. Sturtze stepped off the mound. The tension was palpable in the ballpark. Staring in, he got the sign and delivered. Another splitter, this time, low and away, and Cabrera laid off. 2–2 now. Posada came out to talk to Sturtze so that they could make certain they were in agreement on what to throw. Sturtze came inside with another fastball, and Cabrera fouled it off again.

Another fastball. This time it was low and inside, and Cabrera had worked the count full. Ramirez loomed on deck. Finally, on the ninth pitch of the at-bat, Sturtze missed high and inside, and Cabrera headed to first with a well-earned walk. The at-bat lasted over six minutes.

Torre went out to pull Sturtze and bring in Tom Gordon. Gordon was Torre's second-best relief pitcher behind the incomparable Mariano Rivera. When the Yankees won a championship in 1996, Rivera was the setup man to closer John Wetteland. Rivera eventually became the closer and Torre used other relievers like Mike Stanton to set up Rivera. Now Tom Gordon was the primary setup man entrusted to get the game to Rivera.

Gordon, whose son Dee Strange-Gordon would become a two-time all-star after reaching the majors in 2011, was just 5'9" tall and weighed no more than 165 pounds, but he could bring it. He featured a dynamite fastball and a sharp "12-6" curve, or one that breaks straight down from the 12 o'clock position to the 6. He was a starter from the outset of his career in Kansas City in 1988 all the way through his first years-plus with Boston. The Red Sox had acquired him before the 1996 season and during the 1997 season turned him into a reliever. He saved 11 games for Boston that year, and then in 1998, he became the full-time closer. He made the all-star team for the first time in his career, saving a league-leading 46 games, pitching to a 2.72 ERA, and striking out nearly nine batters per nine innings.

He arrived in New York before the 2004 season, after having pitched with the Cubs and Astros following his four-year stint with Boston. Gordon was Torre's workhorse in 2004, pitching in a whopping 80 games. As a point of comparison, Minnesota's Mike Marshall and Toronto's Mark Eichorn hold the record for most relief appearances in a season with 89. In those games, Torre asked him to throw 89.2 innings, a lot for a person in his role. But he was good—damned good. He had a 2.21 ERA and struck out 10.3 batters per nine innings. He was steady, solid, and often overpowering.

Part of Torre's rationale for making the move mid-inning here was because the next hitter was Manny Ramirez. Ramirez had eight home runs lifetime off Sturtze, but Gordon fared well against him. Lifetime to that point, Ramirez was just 6–35 (.171) off Gordon with one homer. It was a simple matter of matchups. Torre knew the advantage he had matching against Ramirez, rather than allowing Sturtze to face the dangerous right-handed slugger.

Gordon came in to face one of the best hitters in baseball, who was up with a chance to give Boston the lead with one swing of the bat. Ramirez waved his bat and "Flash"—Gordon's long-time nickname—peered in under the bill of his cap, pulled down low just over his eyes. He kicked and fired a dart that Ramirez fouled back for strike one on a wicked cut.

"Quite a rip by Manny Ramirez, who's gone two for three," commented O'Brien.

"Manny Ramirez…unloads on strike one," Buck said on FOX.

"Almost left his shoes," McCarver said.

"Power against power," said Sutcliffe. "Ninety-five mile an hour fastball. A bat that hit forty-three home runs this year. The go-ahead run at home plate." Playoff baseball—especially Yankee-Red Sox playoff baseball—was just so intense. Boston fans nervously chanted, urging Ramirez to launch one.

Gordon had been used in every game of the series so far. He had given up two runs in two-thirds of an inning in Game 1, a hit and no runs in two-thirds of an inning in Game 2, a hit and no runs in an inning in Game 3, and just a walk in two innings in Game 4. Because of the shift in the game schedule due to the earlier rainout, this was his third straight day getting work in, after 17 pitches in Game 3 and 26 in Game 4. Would fatigue be a factor? Torre gambled that it wasn't. He didn't want the series to go back to New York, and if they won Game 5, his bullpen could get several precious days off to rest and recover.

Gordon's second pitch was a slider that missed low and away for a ball. On the 1–1 pitch, Gordon hung a slider belt-high and right over the heart of the plate, and Ramirez just missed it. He banged his hand on his helmet in frustration. Leiter said, "He hung that! Looked like a hanging slider right there. Two pitches now Gordon got away with. First pitch fastball, and that's just a hanging slider, almost too high for Manny to get to. Those are two pitches that Gordon knows he got away with."

The 1–2 pitch was a fastball that missed way too high, and the count drew even at two balls, two strikes.

"Many times after a high fastball comes the breaking ball in the dirt, in this case to Manny down and away," Leiter said.

Sutcliffe commented, "Joe Torre would love a ground ball double play. The fans of the Boston Red Sox are thinking of another kind of double."

Ramirez called time and stepped out and reset. Gordon stared in. Instead of a curve, it was a 94 mph fastball belt high and Ramirez, late on the pitch, fouled it off to the right and out of play. Another hittable pitch that Gordon got away with.

O'Brien noted, "These last two nights and Game 2 typify the kind of games that these two teams have played for the last couple of years. Tense, taut, right down to the wire. Last night came down to the final swing. That's the way Red Sox-Yankees are supposed to be."

Now Gordon threw the curve, and Ramirez hit a routine ground ball to the left of Rodriguez at third. He took a couple of steps over, easily fielded it, fired to Cairo at second, who made the pivot and the throw to first to complete the 5-4-3 double play to end the inning. Cabrera slid hard into Cairo, knocking him backward with substantial force, but Cairo hung in there to make the turn. With David Ortiz on deck, this was just about the worst possible outcome. Even a strikeout would have been preferable. Bellhorn, who led off with a double, never advanced even a single base.

The Fenway crowd was deflated. With Gordon and then Rivera looming in the bullpen, this may have been their best chance to keep the series going and keep hope alive. In one swing, Ramirez' double-play ball ended that.

It was on to the eighth inning. New York was six outs away from eliminating the Red Sox for the second consecutive season and advancing to the World Series.

8

THE EIGHTH INNING

So often in baseball, a squander by one team is followed by the other team scoring the very next time up. Boston had a great chance to cut into New York's lead in the seventh and even had a real possibility of tying the game or taking the lead with one big swing of Manny Ramirez' bat. But Tom Gordon escaped, and the Yankees exhaled and came up to bat looking to add insurance runs and put Boston away.

Timlin stayed on to face Cairo, Jeter, and Rodriguez. Cairo led off and ripped the first pitch he saw into deep left center. It one-hopped the Green Monster. Damon tracked it down and quickly got it to Cabrera, but Cairo had a stand-up double to start the inning.

At this point, the Yankees had two main options. Old-school baseball dictated a sacrifice bunt by Jeter, which could advance Cairo to third, which would have meant that a productive out could have scored a crucial insurance run. But the modern game is played differently.

Baseball statistician Tom Tango has done great work helping to explain the mathematics of baseball. One question that comes up all the time is: Given the current situation, how many runs can we expect to score? And if we bunt here and move a runner along, how many runs can we expect to score in that situation? If the second situation has a lower run expectancy than the first, bunting makes little sense. Why, after all, put yourself in a situation that reduces the number of runs you can expect to score?

Statisticians have analyzed literally hundreds of thousands of baseball games to determine the expected runs in any given situation, based on real-world data. There are three primary situations where managers typically call for a sacrifice (this is not counting when a pitcher is up, in which case sacrificing is almost always the normal—and correct—play). The first is when there's nobody out and a runner at first. Managers will sacrifice in order to move the runner to second—"scoring position"—in the hopes that one of the following hitters will get a single. That single likely will drive the runner in. But hits of any kind are hard to come by in baseball—even the best batters make outs far more than they get hits.

In the case of a runner at first and nobody out, the expected runs are 0.86. That is, if you get a runner at first to lead off the inning, you can expect, over time, to score 0.86 runs. This is because even though he's another base farther from home, there are still three outs to play with, which means more opportunities for an extra-base hit or a play that can extend the inning. But if you sacrifice the runner to second, your expected runs drops to 0.66. In other words, you're not only sacrificing an out, you're sacrificing 20 percent of a chance to score a run in the process. Outs are the most precious currency in the game. Normally, a full nine-inning game provides 27 outs to spend. Giving away outs to marginally increase your chances of scoring a run is generally bad business, but it's especially bad business if it *decreases* your chances of scoring.

A second case where we often see sacrifice bunts is when there's a runner at second with no outs, and he is sacrificed to third, where he can score without the benefit of a hit. This is the situation the Yankees were in after Cairo's double.

Run expectancy tells a different story. If you have a runner at second with nobody out, you can expect to score 1.10 runs. But if you have a runner at third with one out, you can expect to score 0.95 runs. Yes, in fact, a sacrifice in this situation yields fewer expected runs than a runner at second and nobody out. By Tango's methodology, Boston's win expectancy would actually *rise* marginally if Torre elected to have Jeter sacrifice Cairo to third.

By the strict mathematics, Joe Torre's best play, especially with Jeter, Rodriguez, and Sheffield due up, was to leave Cairo at second and take three shots at getting him in.

The third most common scenario is when you have runners at first and second and nobody out. In that situation, your expected runs are 1.44, but if you bunt them over, now you're looking at runners at second and third with one out, and your expected runs drop to 1.38. A small drop, but a drop nonetheless.

The bunt has a long and complicated history in the game of baseball. It showed up first in the early years of the game, in the 1870s, and fans criticized it as being unmanly. The *Boston Globe* in 1873 called bunting "the black game" (not in reference to skin tone but rather that bunting was a sign that a hitter knew he wasn't very good and had to resort to trickery).

President William Taft joined the chorus in 1904, saying that fans should see players "hit it out for all that is in them." In the movie *Moneyball*, Oakland A's general manager Billy Beane, played by Brad Pitt, shares with his players his philosophy on bunting. He says, "No bunting whatsoever. And if someone bunts on us, just pick it up and throw it to first. Don't try to be a hero and go to second. Let them make the mistakes. And when your enemy's making mistakes, don't interrupt them. They're giving you an out, man, they're just giving it to you. Take it and say thank you."

But even teams that understand the statistical reality behind bunting will bunt more in the playoffs than the regular season. Jeter, for example, bunted twice as often in the postseason (as a rate stat) than in the regular season. Teams play more "small ball" in the postseason, falling back on traditional thinking and run manufacturing than during the regular season. Part of this may have to do with the notion that they're facing better pitching in the postseason, making it more difficult to score runs. Therefore, bunting and sacrificing and making productive outs become more important.

Whatever Torre's rationale was, he decided to have Jeter bunt. Just as McCarver said, "He could be bunting here," and pointed out that Jeter had executed a sacrifice bunt the game before, Timlin spun around to bluff a throw to second, trying to keep Cairo close to the bag. Any extra step Cairo could get toward third would make it more likely he could advance safely on a sacrifice.

"I think you give up too much by bunting here, however," McCarver said. "Jeter's natural stroke is the other way. Millar's in [at first]." The idea, of course, is that with Jeter especially, his preference for going to the right side of the field—like he did in his previous at-bat on the three-run double—meant that even if he hit the ball on the ground at an infielder, that would be enough to get Cairo to third. So why not try to get a hit to right field, knowing that even if it resulted in an out, it would accomplish the same thing as giving yourself up in a sacrifice bunt.

Timlin delivered, and Jeter squared to bunt. The pitch was low and Jeter let it go by for ball one. Sutcliffe pointed out how, with the infield in to deal with a sacrifice, huge holes opened up if Jeter were to swing away. But he squared around again and bunted a chopper in front of the mound. Timlin fielded it, took a quick glance at third, realized he had no play there, and took the safe out at first.

Torre played his card and now had Cairo at third with one out and Rodriguez coming up. The previous game, in the eleventh inning, the Yankees had roughly the same scenario. In a tie game, Cairo had led off with a single, and Jeter advanced him to second with a sacrifice. Rodriguez had the chance to drive him in but lined out to short. After Sheffield and Matsui walked, Bernie Williams flied out to end the threat. This time, Rodriguez came up only needing a fly ball to get Cairo in.

Boston brought the infield in, hoping to cut off a ground ball and prevent Cairo from scoring. Advanced metrics are helpful in this situation as well. On balls put in play, batters hit .296 with the infield at regular depth, but the runner from third scores 63 percent of the time. When the infield is in, batters hit .366, a huge increase in the likelihood of a hit—however, the run scores from third only 49 percent of the time.

Timlin's first pitch was a strike. He missed with the next pitch to even the count. Boston could ill afford to let this run in. Overcoming a two-run deficit would be hard enough against Gordon and Rivera. Rodriguez was a more than proficient run-producer. During the 2004 season, he had come up with a runner on third with less than two out some 30 times. In those situations, he batted .333 with a .413 on-base percentage and a 1.046 OPS. Moreover, he drove in 31 runs in those 30 opportunities. He was the right man for New York to have up at the plate.

On the 1–1 pitch, Timlin missed again to make the count two balls and one strike. The difference in baseball between 2–1 and 1–2 is dramatic. For Rodriguez, his odds improved dramatically with that one change in the count. In 2004, with a 1–2 count, he hit .142 with a .148 on-base percentage and .412 OPS in 106 at-bats. But when he got the count to 2–1, he hit .476 with a .477 on-base percentage and 1.239 OPS in 42 at-bats. Timlin missing on the third pitch put him in a huge hole. Rodriguez' OPS jumped to 1.528 on a 3–1 count but back down to a .587 OPS on a 2–2 count. The next pitch was huge.

Buck said, "Timlin pitched a scoreless seventh. He's going to have to do some work to pitch a scoreless eighth after the double by Cairo."

Timlin threw his best pitch of the night, an 85 mph slider low and away that Rodriguez hacked at and missed. On the 2–2 pitch, Timlin fired a fastball high and tight that Rodriguez swung at and missed for strike three.

"Mike Timlin just found a hole," Sutcliffe said. "He went up and in to get ahead in the count and finished him off in the exact same spot."

Sheffield was next, and Timlin was not out of trouble, but now New York needed a hit or an error to get Cairo in instead of just a routine fly ball out. Timlin's first pitch missed for ball one. Matsui was waiting on deck, and Timlin did not want to have to deal with the Yankee left fielder with two runners on base. Timlin missed again for another ball. His third pitch also missed, and the count was 3–0.

"We talked about it last night," Buck commented. "You have a shot, if you're the Red Sox, for as good as Gordon has been, your shot may come in the bottom of the eighth inning, with Rivera at the moment seated in the Yankee bullpen."

No pitcher wanted to groove a fat pitch to Sheffield, particularly in the playoffs. But interestingly, Sheffield almost never swung on a 3–0 count. In 35 plate appearances with a 3–0 count this year, Sheffield only had one official at-bat, meaning most of the time, he took on 3–0. He had 34 walks—7 intentional—in those 35 plate appearances, and recorded one out.

Timlin hit the inside corner with a fastball that in other circumstances Sheffield may have launched into orbit. Now it was 3–1, and this was a count Sheffield enjoyed, batting .375 with a 1.453 OPS in these situations. Timlin still had to be very careful. His next pitch was even better, more on the inside corner at the knees. Sheffield leaned back away from the plate, and Kellogg barked out a strike. Sheffield, unhappy with Kellogg, turned to voice his complaint. A replay showed that Sheffield was right— the ball just missed the inside corner. Timlin caught a little break, and now the count was 3–2.

It didn't matter, as the next pitch was high and inside, and Sheffield drew the walk, bringing up Matsui.

Francona came to the mound, removing Timlin and bringing in ace reliever Keith Foulke.

Foulke had been a terrific reliever for years, first with the White Sox and then with the Athletics. He faced Boston in the 2003 AL Divisional series, which Boston won in five tense games. Boston brought him over following that season, and he was phenomenal for the Red Sox in 2004, pitching to a 2.17 ERA and saving 32 games. He was tough as nails, durable, and he didn't put many runners on base, posting his second straight season with a WHIP under 1.00. He did not have a big arm, able to get his fastball up to 90 on occasion, but sitting normally between 87 and 89. His gift was his control, his changeup, and his will. He just did not give in, and he would fight tooth and nail in every at-bat.

He had pitched 83 innings for Boston during the season—almost as many as Gordon's impressive number of 89.2—and in the playoffs to this point, he had thrown 6.2 innings, allowing just two hits and no runs while striking out nine batters. In Game 4, he had pitched 2.2 innings of gritty relief, keeping New York off the board and giving Boston a chance to make a comeback. He was in to face Matsui, whom he faced twice the night before. The first time was in the seventh inning, and Foulke induced a groundout to first. The second time was in the ninth inning, and Foulke struck him out.

It was imperative to keep New York off the board. Foulke's first pitch was a letter-high fastball at 85 miles an hour. Matsui couldn't resist and swung and missed for strike one. Sutcliffe commented that MLB officials already had the series MVP trophy sitting outside Matsui's locker in the ninth inning of Game 4.

Another fastball drifted outside, and Matsui laid off to make the count 1-1. Matsui was only 1-7 in his career against Foulke, so Francona liked the matchup. Another elevated fastball that Matsui missed made it one ball and two strikes, and the Fenway fans rose to their feet, urging Foulke on to get this last out.

Foulke stepped off the rubber to collect himself. Nervousness reigned in Fenway. Foulke stepped back on, got the sign from Varitek, and came set. He fired a fastball right on the outside corner that Kellogg called a ball, as it apparently just missed by millimeters. Varitek held his glove there for an extra second, framing it for Foulke, who hit Varitek's glove perfectly. No dice. The count was 2–2. Replay showed that Kellogg got the call right.

Foulke nearly hit Matsui with the next pitch, and Matsui jackknifed out of the way. The count was full, which meant that Sheffield would be on the move with the pitch. That meant that if Matsui hit one into the gap, Sheffield likely would score all the way from first.

Sox fans pounded the side wall on the infield. Matsui dug in. Foulke stared in and got the sign. Matsui lifted an 84 mph changeup to left field. Ramirez sprinted in and made a running backhanded catch for the third out of the inning. Torre had bunted to get Cairo to third instead of letting Jeter swing away, and New York came up empty.

DUE UP FOR the Red Sox in the bottom of the eighth were Ortiz, Millar, and Nixon. Torre had said that Rivera was available to pitch but that he did not want to start the eighth inning with Rivera. So Gordon was coming back out to pitch, but Rivera was warming up. New York had six outs to get, with an 81 percent chance of winning the game.

Torre had been sensing that Gordon was nervous. Jim Baumbach, in a February 2005 piece for *Newsday*, would write, reflecting back on the 2004 ALCS, that "the playoff atmosphere clearly got the best of Gordon. An excitable competitor who has no need for pregame pep talks, Gordon had trouble dealing with his emotions on the postseason stage, and Torre often described his mound presence during the ALCS as 'jumpy.' The nervous energy Gordon used to his advantage in the regular season became something he no longer could channel, and his failures put even more pressure on Rivera. Gordon was caught up in the moment, saying at the time that he had trouble falling asleep before daybreak some days. It showed in his lack of location and forced Torre to bring in Rivera much earlier than he wanted to against the Red Sox."

Torre would later comment that Gordon "was excited about the opportunity last year [2004] and had trouble controlling the emotions. It wasn't that he was afraid. He was excited." Stories circulated that before Game 6 of the ALCS, just one day after the epic Game 5, Gordon threw up, a bundle of nerves.

Prior to 2004, Gordon's postseason résumé was suspect. In 1998, he pitched twice in the divisional round for Boston against Cleveland. He gave up four hits, four walks, and three runs in just three innings against the Indians, including a disastrous blown save in Game 4 that ultimately cost the Red Sox the series. In 1999, he faced Cleveland and New York in five games, pitching four innings and allowing four hits, two walks, a hit batter, and four runs. Over the course of those two years, he gave up 15 base-runners and seven runs over just seven innings. He gave up runs in five of his seven postseason appearances, and before 2004, he had yet to get through a single postseason appearance without allowing either a run or a base runner.

He had reason to be nervous. Not only was his postseason track record spotty at best, but he was going up against Big Papi.

By 2004, David Ortiz was already a terrific hitter for the Red Sox. In 2003 and 2004 combined, he hit .295 with an OPS of .973 and an OPS+ of 144. Over 278 games, he had 86 doubles, 72 homers, and 240 RBIs. In his last 10 postseason games dating back to Game 5 of the 2004 ALCS, Ortiz had hit .476 with a 1.361 OPS, with three homers and 14 RBIs. David Ortiz was great, but he wasn't yet DAVID ORTIZ.

The former was excellent, but the latter became otherworldly. His otherworldliness began the night before, or technically, in the wee hours of that morning, when he won Game 4 with a walk-off homer to keep Boston alive. In Boston's 2007 World Series run, he would hit .370 with a 1.204 OPS, three homers, and 14 RBIs. In their 2013 World Series run, he would hit .353 with a 1.206 OPS, five homers, and 13 RBIs, including a monumental grand slam in the eighth inning of Game 2 of the ALCS to tie the game and give Boston life. In the World Series that year, he put up absolutely preposterous numbers, coming up to bat 25 times, getting 11 hits, drawing eight walks, hitting two homers, and posting a .688 average, a .760 on-base percentage, and a 1.948 OPS. Video game stuff when you've input a cheat code.

In three World Series', Ortiz would hit .455, with a .576 on-base percentage, a 1.372 OPS, hit three homers, drive in 14 runs, and score 14 runs, all in just 14 games. He would produce clutch hit after clutch hit over his career.

In Game 4 of the 2003 AL Divisional Series against Oakland, Ortiz came up in the bottom of the eighth inning to face none other than Keith Foulke, with Boston down two games to one and facing elimination, and down 4–3 in the game. There were two outs, Garciaparra on third and Ramirez on first. On a 3–2 pitch, Ortiz doubled to score both runners and give Boston the lead. They'd go on to win that game, and then Game 5 in Oakland, to reach the ALCS against New York.

In Game 3 of the 2004 AL Divisional Series against Anaheim, the score was tied 6–6 in the bottom of the tenth inning. Anaheim had lefty Jarrod Washburn on the mound, and Ortiz strode to the plate with two outs and one runner on. Washburn threw a curve on the first pitch, and Ortiz launched it over the Green Monster for a walk-off game-winning (and series-winning) home run.

In Game 4 of the 2004 ALCS, Ortiz gave Boston the lead in the fifth inning with a two-run single, and then in the twelfth inning hit a game-winning walk-off two-run home run off Paul Quantrill to keep Boston in the series and bring them to this Game 5.

In Game 7 of the 2004 ALCS, Boston, trying to complete the comeback from an 0–3 deficit in games, got a quick start as Damon singled and stole second. Ramirez hit a single to shallow left, and Damon tried to score but got gunned down at the plate on a beautiful relay from Matsui-to-Jeter-to-Posada. It seemed like Boston was back to being the Boston that failed in big moments on the biggest stage against the hated Yankees, but Ortiz came up and on the first pitch he saw, he launched a two-run homer to right field. Buck said on the FOX broadcast, "You talk about picking up your ball club…After losing a runner at the plate…Ortiz has done that all year, all October, and he goes deep to put Boston out in front." Just when the Yankees were restoring order, Ortiz immediately gave momentum back to the Red Sox.

In the 2013 ALCS against Detroit, Boston was down 1–0 in games, down 5–1 in the eighth inning of Game 2, and was due to face the incomparable Justin Verlander in Game 3. The bases were loaded, and Ortiz launched a grand slam off Joaquin Benoit to tie the game and give Boston life. They'd go on to win the game, the series, and then beat the Cardinals in six games in the 2013 World Series.

Only two players in baseball history have more walk-off hits than Ortiz' 20: Frank Robinson with 26 and Dusty Baker with 21. Neither of those players ever had a postseason walk-off hit. Nobody else in baseball history has more than two walk-off hits in postseason play. David Ortiz had four. Derek Jeter, who is a legend for his clutch hitting, only had seven walk-off hits in his career, and just one in all his postseason games.

Ortiz was born in his native Dominican Republic in 1975. Signed by Seattle in 1992, he was listed in their organization as David Arias, which was the last name of his mother, Ángela Rosa Arias. He looked up to Ramon and Pedro Martínez. Minnesota traded for him in 1996, and there he chose to be called David Ortiz, taking the last name of his father, Enrique. Sportswriter Jay Jaffe joked about the name change, saying that Ortiz was "literally the player to be named later."

Pedro would later go to bat for Ortiz, suggesting to Boston management that they acquire the blossoming slugger.

Ortiz endeared himself to Boston fans throughout his playing career for his on-field exploits. But one of his most memorable moments came in the wake of a terrible incident. In 2013, Dzhokhar Tsarnaev and Tamerlan Tsarnaev, brothers from Chechnya, denotated bombs in the crowd at the Boston Marathon, killing three people and wounding hundreds more. In their attempt to elude capture, they also shot a police officer from MIT. The brothers were captured days later, and in a pregame speech to the Fenway faithful before Boston's game with the Royals on April 20, David Ortiz thanked Boston police for their efforts to nab the terrorists. In front of 35,000 people, he said, "This is our fucking city. And nobody's going to dictate our freedom. Stay strong."

The city adopted a motto following the terrorist attack: Boston Strong. The FCC, meanwhile, had to decide what to do with FOX, who showed the speech, including Ortiz' use of the forbidden F-word. Then-FCC chairman Julius Genachowski said in a tweet, "David Ortiz spoke from the heart at today's Red Sox game. I stand with Big Papi and the people of Boston."

Hollywood Reporter writer Aaron Couch noted, "If ever there were an excuse for on-air F-bomb, this is it." The Red Sox used "Boston Strong" as a slogan for the rest of the year, and when they won the World Series, Dave O'Brien said, "The 2013 Red Sox are the World Champions! And Boston Strong!"

Ortiz became an immortal athlete and citizen in the city of Boston, not only for his success but for his popularity. He nearly became victim himself to a terrible tragedy several years later, however. On June 9, 2019, while at the Dial Bar and Lounge in East Santo Domingo, Ortiz suffered serious wounds from a gunshot attack. The attacker got off a motorcycle and ambushed him, causing multiple injuries. Ortiz was rushed to the hospital and had a six-hour operation to remove portions of his intestines, colon, and gallbladder. The next day, the Red Sox, for whom he did not work anymore, sent a medical flight to take him to Boston, where he would be furnished with world-class medical care at Mass General. Authorities determined that he was not the target of the attack but was simply in the wrong place at the wrong time. Ortiz' healing took time, but he eventually made a full recovery. On September 9, he threw out the ceremonial first pitch at Fenway.

Most of Ortiz' heroics and the experiences that would make him a legend were still in the future when he stepped to the plate to lead off the bottom of the eighth inning against Tom Gordon. Before the MLB broadcast crew went to the break between half innings, O'Brien said, "Ortiz is coming up. After his heroics last night, does he have more left in him?"

Gordon's first pitch was a biting fastball at the knees on the outer half of the plate for strike one. Buck commented, "Joe Torre rode this Yankee bullpen all the way into the postseason, and he will ride it throughout."

On MLB, Sutcliffe said, "They [Boston] have a long ways to go, and as the song goes, a short time to get there. They are down to their final six outs if they plan on celebrating anymore."

Gordon fired pitch number two, a low fastball in the same spot as the first pitch. Ortiz swung and made contact. The ball left his bat and soared deep to left center.

"High fly ball...deep into the night...way, way back, and gone! Off the Volvo sign! Ortiz does it again! This home run draws the Red Sox to within one!" O'Brien excitedly called.

Fenway Park erupted. New York still had the lead, but suddenly Boston had life. Ortiz shot adrenaline into the veins of the fans and team alike, and Fenway was shaking. Ortiz rounded the bases slowly.

"He is really something," Trupiano said on WEEI. "David Ortiz signed a multiyear contract this year with the Red Sox...he has come up with some of the biggest hits over the last two years for the club."

Gordon got a new baseball from Kellogg and began walking around the mound rubbing it up. He was trying to refocus. He still had a job to do. Ortiz had done his. A fan held up a sign that said, "Believe in Boston." Ortiz hit home plate, tapped his chest, and raised his hands to the sky, his home run tradition.

"He wore out the Yankees all year long," Sutcliffe said. "You'd like to have had him up there with a couple of men on like last inning. It didn't happen...his good buddy Manny Ramirez hit into a double play. Now Mariano Rivera will start to crank it up."

"What a dynamic, clutch hitter this guy has been for the last two years for the Boston Red Sox," said McCarver.

Boston still had work to do. For all of Ortiz' heroics, they were still behind, with six outs left. The score was identical to the night before, 4–3 Yankees, and New York had their best pitcher getting ready to come in. Kevin Millar came up, hoping to duplicate what he did the night before—get on base, any way possible.

Gordon started Millar off with a slider that Millar, thinking fastball, missed by a mile. Pitchers often throw fastballs to the next hitter after giving up a home run, and Millar guessed that Gordon would as well. Strike one. He threw another one, this time off the outer part of the plate. Millar checked his swing, but Kellogg indicated that he went, and suddenly Millar was down 0–2.

Gordon bounced the next pitch in the dirt, not remotely tempting Millar. "Let's go Red Sox!" chants reverberated throughout Fenway. Millar called time and stepped out of the box. He gathered himself and settled back in. Gordon fired a big curve that also hit the dirt in front of the plate, and now the count was even at two balls, two strikes. A sharp slider missed outside, and Millar had worked the count full.

The MLB camera flashed to the Boston dugout. Sutcliffe said, "Nice little shot of Dave Roberts there. Ball four, you think we might see him again?" O'Brien replied, "I think there's a pretty good chance."

Gordon missed with a fastball low and inside for ball four, and Millar took first base. Instantly, Dave Roberts sprinted out of the dugout and replaced Millar at first, exactly like the night before.

"This is like seeing the same movie again," quipped McCarver. "Two days in a row."

Stottlemyre came out to visit Gordon. Posada and Gordon were already engaged in conversation as the pitching coach made his way to the mound.

Buck said on FOX, "The question is for Joe Torre and Mel Stottlemyre, obviously, is six outs too much after Mariano worked two outs—rather, two innings—last night?"

O'Brien said on MLB, "He [Roberts] doesn't come into the game unless he's trying to run."

Boston acquired Roberts at the trade deadline in 2004, hoping that his speed and defense would come in handy down the stretch and in key late-inning spots in the playoffs. In his first 309 games from 1999 to 2003, he stole 97 bases against 29 caught stealing, for a steal percentage of 77 percent, which was a little better than the league average of 68.6 percent. He was a threat to run every time he was on base. In 2002, he stole 45 bases, and in 2003, he stole 40. In 2004, he split the season between the Dodgers (33 steals vs. 1 caught stealing) and Boston (5 steals vs. 2 caught stealing). For the season, he was 38 for 41 (92.7 percent) in stolen base attempts. When he had the chance to steal in the ninth inning of Game 4, he took off and barely beat an excellent throw by Posada. That steal set up Bill Mueller's single to center that easily scored the swift Roberts. It would go down in Boston history as the most important and most famous stolen base in franchise history.

"Gordon is very poor at holding base runners," Trupiano said.

"And he can bounce that hard curve of his," Castiglione replied.

Trot Nixon came up and Roberts took his customary large lead off first. The Fenway crowd was loud and amped up. He did not, as it turned out, run on the first pitch—a different approach from the night before—and Gordon pumped a fastball in for strike one.

Rivera looked on from the Yankee bullpen, obviously ready to go. Roberts took his lead, and Gordon threw over, causing Roberts to dive back safely. Gordon did not want Roberts to get a good jump like he got against them the night before.

Gordon toed the rubber again, and Roberts took his lead, his left leg bent, ready to spring into action. He flinched, and Gordon stepped off the rubber and shot Roberts a look. The Red Sox speedster took a step toward first. A huge game of chicken.

"Roberts is gonna go," Buck said. "The question is when."

Another throw to first. Roberts dove back safe. Nixon stepped out and took a deep breath. Red Sox fans screamed loudly. Gordon came to the set as Roberts led again, and this time, Gordon just held the ball. Roberts finally stepped back to first and Gordon came off the rubber.

During the evolution of the game, pitchers found numerous ways to keep fast runners close to first. One way was to throw over—either a "courtesy" throw, which was a soft lob to first, just to let the runner know he's being watched, or a serious pickoff throw, which was a hard dart low and into the path of the runner as he dove back to the base.

A second method is what is called the slide step. Instead of bringing the forward leg high in order to drive forward with maximum power, a pitcher will simply step quickly toward home plate. This throws off the timing of the runner and gets the ball to the catcher more quickly, meaning the runner has less time to steal. In a game where stolen bases are often—as was the case with Roberts the game before—stolen by inches and milliseconds, a slide step could be the difference between safe and out.

A third method is to just hold the ball. McCarver explained, "That's the biggest deterrent to a base runner, is to hold the ball. It throws his timing all off. One of the problems, Al, as you know, it could throw the timing of the pitcher off."

"No question about it," Leiter replied on the FOX broadcast. "The pitcher's thinking anything but making a good pitch to home plate, you'd be off by that much and it could be the difference between a ball being up or in an area in which you didn't want to throw it to. All of this stuff is an absolute distraction for the pitcher. That's what great base runners do. They don't even have to steal."

"I don't think I've ever seen a base runner who looks like he's gonna steal on every single pitch more than Dave Roberts," said McCarver.

"All he's missing is the starting blocks down there," said Buck. "Because he is dug in, ready to go."

Gordon chose to hold the ball, and Roberts grew impatient. Nixon also had to display tremendous patience, as Gordon was paying more attention to the runner than the hitter. Finally Nixon called time.

Trupiano said, "Lou Brock and the great base stealer Maury Wills will tell you that it really bugs them when pitchers hold the ball. That's the best way to make a base stealer edgy. Just hold the ball, disrupt the timing. They're anxious to run."

Posada came out to talk to Gordon. The volume in Fenway Park rose.

"There's no question that Gordon's distracted," Castiglione said.

Gordon fired over to first again. Roberts dove back. The game between the two went on, and Nixon waited for his chance to swing. Finally, Gordon delivered his second pitch, a curve down and in for a ball.

Gordon's next pitch—again Roberts not going—was a fastball that missed low. Gordon's attention was divided, and it was showing.

"It would be so much easier for Joe Torre if he had a left-handed reliever that he trusted. You eliminate the running game. You've got a left-handed reliever facing a left-handed hitter, the percentages favor you. But he has lost confidence in Heredia," Sutcliffe said, referencing Yankee lefty Félix Heredia, who was essentially the Mike Myers of the Yankee bullpen. Heredia had not yet pitched in the series.

Another pitch missed, making the count 3–1.

"There's no question Roberts is in Gordon's head," said Leiter.

"Absolutely," agreed McCarver. "So if you're Nixon, you're looking for a fastball, inside part. A guy who can certainly jerk it around the Pesky Pole in right field."

Rodriguez came over to say a few words to Gordon. "You're going," Sutcliffe said. "There's no reason not to go. If it's a fastball near the zone, Trot Nixon's gonna take a whack at it. If it's something off-speed, he should be able to steal the base easily."

Gordon came to the set. Roberts led. As soon as Gordon's foot came up, Roberts took off for second. Gordon's pitch was indeed a fastball, and Nixon ripped it to center for a base hit. Roberts hit second flying and advanced to third standing as Bernie Williams tossed the ball back into the infield.

"Nixon got his fastball. Roberts to third easily. Oh, the value of speed," McCarver said.

Gabe Kapler came in to run for Nixon, and Boston had excellent speed on the bases. Runners were at first and third, with nobody out, and switch-hitting catcher Jason Varitek coming up. Joe Torre came out and called for Rivera, who entered the game facing a brutally difficult save opportunity.

He would face the Red Sox a ridiculous 115 times over the course of his career, second only to his 136 games versus Baltimore, posting a 13–7 career record with a 2.86 ERA. His ERA against Boston, of course, was tremendous, but it was more than a half-run worse than his career ERA overall.

In the 2004 regular season, Rivera faced Boston nine times, saving three games. But he went 0–2 and blew two saves, and his ERA against the Red Sox was a surprising 4.22. Moreover, his WHIP, which was a 1.00 for his overall career, was 1.50 against Boston during the 2004 campaign. Including Game 4 of the

ALCS, he had blown three saves against Boston. On July 24, Bill Mueller hit a walk-off home run in Fenway to beat Rivera and the Yankees. On September 17, Johnny Damon hit a bloop to center to beat Rivera and the Yankees in New York. And in Game 4 of the ALCS, the Millar walk, Roberts steal, and Mueller single handed Rivera a third blown save at the hands of the Red Sox. It wasn't like they had Rivera's number, but as much as anyone could say that, Boston could.

At a minimum, the Red Sox had some confidence going up against the great Yankee closer. They had seen him so much over the years and had recorded enough success that they could at least believe they could get to him.

In this situation, a save would have been near miraculous. A speedy and smart runner at third, a fast runner at first, and Boston just needed a ground ball or fly out to score Roberts, and because there were no outs, they had two chances to get that done. Rivera would have to be perfect in order to save the game. If anyone could get out of this jam, it was him.

THE SAVE RULE became an official statistic in 1969, but its origins go back further than that. In the dead ball era, teams often had just a few pitchers on the roster, and they were expected to pitch the whole game, regardless of the score. As the game evolved, more pitchers were added, but there were still clearly defined starters and relievers. Generally speaking, you became a reliever if you weren't good enough to be a starter. Now this didn't mean that there weren't excellent relievers. For example, Dick Radatz pitched for the Red Sox from 1962 to 1969, exclusively in relief; and from 1962 to 1964, he was one of the best pitchers in the game. In an era when strikeouts weren't as common, he struck out more than 10 batters per nine innings each of those three seasons, compiling an ERA of 2.17. He was also a workhorse, averaging 138 innings a year over that span. Decades earlier, the 1927 Yankees had Wilcy Moore, who started 12 games and relieved 38 times for New York, winning 19 games and saving 13 over 213 innings.

In the 1970s, the game began to see pitchers like Rollie Fingers, who became relief aces, or "firemen"—pitchers who came in and put out fires left by the starters. They became specialists, and the save was their stock-in-trade statistic.

A save was originally a term used fairly loosely in the game, meant to indicate when a pitcher came in relief with his team ahead and who finished out the game, regardless of score. Sportswriter Jerome Holtzman gave specific criteria for saves in the early '60s, it became an official stat in 1969, and its modern definition was spelled out in 1975, as explained on MLB's official website:

> A save is awarded to the relief pitcher who finishes a game for the winning team, under certain circumstances. A pitcher cannot receive a save and a win in the same game. A relief pitcher recording a save must preserve his team's lead while doing one of the following:
>
> - Enter the game with a lead of no more than three runs and pitch at least one inning.
> - Enter the game with the tying run in the on-deck circle, at the plate or on the bases.
> - Pitch at least three innings.

In the 1990s, Tony La Russa altered the way pitchers were used, creating the left-handed specialist role (LOOGY) and the one-inning save specialist (a "closer"). Every reliever was slotted into his specific role, and usage patterns were predictable and consistent.

The save statistic was meant to capture the contribution relief pitchers made to the game, which was not insignificant. But it began to change the way managers used their players, and it began to change the economics of the game. Fran Zimniuch, in his book, *Fireman: The Evolution of the Closer in Baseball* (2010), pointed out that closers (the ones who accumulate saves) make more money than setup men (the ones who take the lead from the starter to the closer).

In 1996, the Yankees won the World Series with a dynamic back end of the bullpen, featuring Mariano Rivera and John Wetteland. For illustration purposes, consider their statistics:

- Wetteland: 63.2 innings, 2.83 ERA, 1.18 WHIP, 9.8 k/9
- Rivera: 107.2 innings, 2.09 ERA, 0.99 WHIP, 10.9 k/9

Rivera was the better pitcher, by a considerable margin. He pitched more innings (nearly double), and he kept runners off base at a better rate than Wetteland. He struck out more batters per nine innings. He had a lower earned run average. And in terms of the wins above replacement metric, Wetteland was worth 1.2 WAR, while Rivera was worth 3.5 WAR, the most on the entire pitching staff.

John Wetteland, however, made the all-star team, and Rivera did not. Wetteland was making $4 million that year (a princely sum back then for MLB players), while Rivera was making $131,125. Why was Wetteland an all-star while Rivera was not? Why was Wetteland considered the best reliever on the staff while Rivera was number two? Why, when Rivera was clearly—objectively so—the far superior pitcher, and worth nearly three times as much to the Yankees in terms of on-field performance than Wetteland?

The answer is the save statistic. Rivera was "just" the setup man, saving five games that year, while Wetteland was the golden and anointed closer, saving 43 games. This is not to say that saving games is easy. There's immense pressure to perform well or a winnable game is suddenly lost. And make no mistake—Wetteland was a terrific pitcher for New York, but he was not nearly as good as Rivera. And to demonstrate how the save rule changed how managers acted, once Wetteland left after the 1996 season, Rivera became the new closer—getting a "promotion," as it were—and suddenly started pitching fewer innings but accumulating more saves. And making more all-star teams. And more money.

Saves are important, of course. A successful save means that a winnable game has, in fact, been won. A blown save means that oftentimes (but not always), a winnable game has been lost. Obviously, sometimes a relief pitcher blows a save and his team comes back and still wins the game. But accumulating lots of blown saves is generally not a good thing for a bullpen.

Not all saves are equal. By rule, if a pitcher comes into the game with a three-run lead and two outs, but there are two runners on base, and he just gets that last out before three runs score, he gets a save. That's as easy a save as one could ask for. But then there are saves like what Rivera was facing in the eighth inning of Game 5. Boston had a runner at third with nobody out, and Rivera was handed a one-run lead. He had to get three outs while preventing that runner on third from scoring. Moreover, in order to get the save, he'd have to pitch another whole inning to lock the game down.

In other words, there are saves, and there are *saves*, and Rivera was being asked to give the Yankees the latter.

IN ORDER TO do that, he had to first retire Jason Varitek. Varitek was an excellent player for Boston, having a solid season at-bat, but he wasn't a guy fans loved having up in clutch situations. In 2004, he batted just .188 with 11 RBIs in "late and close" situations. However, he was a good hitter for driving in runners from third and less than two out. During the season, he came up on 32 occasions in those situations and drove the run in 16 times. He didn't need a hit. Just a modest fly ball into the outfield.

Rivera, the ultimate escape artist, peered in to get the sign from Posada. He came to his set and then uncoiled his long, lanky frame, firing a 92 mph fastball well outside the zone high and away for ball one. The crowd noise went up a notch.

"After pitching two innings, literally this morning, Mariano Rivera is back in it in the eighth inning, trying to keep it 4–3 New York," Buck said on FOX.

"You gotta be smart," Sutcliffe said. "You gotta remember that the pitcher is in trouble here, not you."

Rivera's next pitch was a cut fastball that moved down and in for another ball, and suddenly Varitek was up in the count, 2–0. In the driver's seat, if anyone ever could be there against the superlative Rivera.

Beginning on July 24 of 2004, Rivera had faced Boston six times during the regular season and playoffs. He was 0–2 with a 7.36 ERA, and he was just three for six in save chances. This one was the most important, and most difficult, of them all.

"Two and oh," said Buck, "with Rivera's nemesis, Bill Mueller, on deck."

Boston fans alternatively held their breath or screamed at the top of their lungs, urging Varitek to deliver the run. Fans banged on the side walls of the ballpark in a steady rhythm. Rivera dug into the rubber and once again looked in to Posada for the sign. Varitek wiggled his bat, staring out at Rivera, waiting for what he hoped was a good pitch to hit.

Rivera unleashed a fastball on the outer part of the plate and Varitek lifted a high fly ball to center. It wasn't deep, and Bernie Williams had no trouble tracking it for the out, but it was deep enough to score Roberts, as Williams tossed it in to second base to make sure that Kapler didn't advance.

Tyler Kepner wrote in the game report in the next day's *New York Times*, "It was almost an impossible situation for Rivera, and he could not avoid a blown save. Varitek hit a sacrifice fly to center, tying the score, 4–4. It was Rivera's third blown save in five chances this postseason; he had converted 30 of 32 before this year."

Mueller stepped into the box next, and Boston had hopes for another run. He had stung Rivera twice during the season already, once beating him with a walk-off home run in July, and then again in the ninth inning of Game 4 when he drove home Roberts. Rivera still had work to do.

The first pitch was a biting cutter down and in that Mueller fouled off out of play to the left. Rivera did not have to worry about Kapler running. He wasn't much of a stolen base threat. But Kapler did possess enough speed to score from first on a double, so the Yankees were guarding against that possibility.

Kapler took a modest lead, and Posada set up inside, the typical path for Rivera's cut fastball—in on lefties. He indeed threw the cutter, and as was so often the case when he faced left-handed hitters, the pitch bore in on Mueller's hands and broke his bat. Mueller hit a soft chopper to first that Clark fielded. He had no play at second, so he stepped on first to easily retire Mueller.

Bellhorn was next, and he had swung the bat well thus far in Game 5, with two hard-hit balls to second for outs and then a solid double to lead off the seventh. He worked the count full before Rivera struck him out to end the inning, but the damage was done. Boston had rallied once again off New York's superlative bullpen, this time to tie the game at four.

Neil Keefe wrote in his book, *The Next Yankees Era: My Transition From the Core Four to the Baby Bombers*, "Rivera got Varitek to fly out to center, but Roberts scored on the sacrifice, tying the game and handing Rivera a 'blown save' to show how ridiculous and dumb that stat is. Mueller grounded out and Bellhorn struck out swinging. Rivera had retired all three batters he faced in the inning, but would be forever credited with 'blowing' it. The Red Sox had scored twice, the two-run lead was gone and my counting the remaining outs had stopped."

On to the ninth, with Keith Foulke looking to keep the game tied.

9

THE NINTH INNING

When Doug Mientkiewicz woke up on the morning of July 31, 2004, he was a member of the Minnesota Twins, and he was preparing for a game that night against the Boston Red Sox. The night before, Boston had drubbed the Twins, 8–2, but Mientkiewicz had a terrific night, going 3–3 with two runs batted in. He was preparing to face sinker-baller Derek Lowe, who was going up against righty Brad Radke.

Meanwhile, Nomar Garciaparra was preparing to face Radke, as the Sox were looking to gain ground on the Yankees in the AL East. Minnesota was in a divisional race of their own in the AL Central.

Orlando Cabrera had the day off, his Montreal Expos having come off a victory in Florida over the defending champion, but now dismantled, Florida Marlins the previous night. The Expos wouldn't play until August 1.

It was the day of MLB's trade deadline, and teams like the Red Sox were looking to make final moves for the playoff push over the last two months of the season. Rumors naturally swirled around Boston, and the players were a little on edge. One rumor had Lowe being traded, and even though he was the scheduled starting pitcher, he wasn't in the Sox' locker room. People wondered why.

At 2:45 central time, backup catcher Doug Mirabelli said in the clubhouse, "Fifteen minutes to go, and we're all still here."

Five minutes later, Manny Ramirez said, "Ten minutes to go, and I'm still here. I guess I'm not going anywhere."

At 3:45 central time, a little over two hours before first pitch, Garciaparra, already in uniform, was summoned into Terry Francona's office. There, he took a phone call from general manager Theo Epstein, who told Garciaparra that he had been traded to the Chicago Cubs. He took the news like a pro, letting his teammates know and spending a few minutes hugging them and wishing them well.

"You've got to keep it going, man," Ramirez told him as they embraced.

Garciaparra later told reporters, "If it was in my control, I'd still be wearing a Red Sox uniform. That's the place I know, love, all those fans, I'll always remember. But I'm also going to another great place, a phenomenal city with great tradition as well." The Cubs were having a solid season, and they'd finish with 89 wins, but far behind division-winning St. Louis, who won 105 on the season.

Cabrera was similarly informed that he was going to Boston, and Mientkiewicz was told by management that he, too, was headed to the Red Sox. For Cabrera, this meant a flight during his day off to meet up with the team, but for Mientkiewicz, it meant a quick change of uniform and a short walk across the field to meet his new teammates.

Theo Epstein said afterward, "We lost a great player in Nomar Garciaparra, but we've made our club more functional. We weren't going to win a World Series with our defense." Mientkiewicz was a skilled first baseman, even though he was weak at the plate, and Cabrera offered a defensive upgrade at shortstop. Mientkiewicz promptly started for Boston against his former team and went 2–4 with a run scored in a 5–4 loss to the Twins.

Over the next week or so, Mientkiewicz started regularly, but mid-month, Terry Francona began to use him more in a bench role, as a left-handed pinch-hitter and as a late-inning defensive replacement for Kevin Millar, who was a much better hitter and much worse fielder. Mientkiewicz would produce very little at the plate the rest of the season, hitting just .215 but providing Gold Glove–caliber defense. The move did precisely what Theo Epstein had hoped it would.

When Roberts ran for Millar in Game 4, Mueller singled him home, bringing up Bellhorn. Francona sent Mientkiewicz, a worse hitter but a better stick-handler, in to pinch-hit for Bellhorn. Playing for just one run, he had Mientkiewicz sacrifice bunt, and the former Twin did his job, successfully advancing Mueller to second. Damon reached on an error to put runners at first and third, and Boston had a chance to end Game 4 right there, but Cabrera struck out, Ramirez walked to load the bases, and Ortiz popped out to second. Mientkiewicz would play first, and Pokey Reese would come in to the fifth spot in the order but play second base. The game would go to the twelfth inning with Boston winning in a classic.

In Game 5, the moves were much simpler. Millar walked, Roberts pinch-ran for him, and after the inning was over, Mientkiewicz simply replaced Roberts and played first. It wouldn't take long for Mientkiewicz to get some action. On Foulke's first pitch of the inning, a soft 74 mph change, Bernie Williams reached out and popped weakly to Mientkiewicz, who made the routine play just in foul territory for the first out.

Jorge Posada was next. Foulke started him off with a fastball high and outside for ball one. Another fastball, this one at 85 mph, dotted the outside corner for a strike. Foulke then missed with a slider down and in, somehow avoiding making contact with Posada, to make the count 2–1. Foulke then got Posada to hit another weak pop-up to first, this time barely in fair territory, and Mientkiewicz once again made an easy catch for the second out of the inning.

Rubén Sierra was next, and he was having a good night. He was three for three, with three singles, a walk, and a run scored. At thirty-seven years of age, Sierra was a thoroughly professional hitter. Foulke knew he had to be careful.

Foulke's first pitch, a slow change, missed outside for ball one. He then pumped a fastball on the outside corner for a strike to even the count. Foulke's fastball was well below average, anywhere from 84 to 87 miles an hour, but it stood in sharp contrast to his great changeup, which he threw in the mid-70s. The 10 mph difference in velocity was enough to throw the hitter's timing way off. Additionally, Foulke had terrific command of his pitches and could spot his fastball wherever he wanted. His slow fastball, great changeup repertoire was not too dissimilar from that of the great Koji Uehara, who closed games for Boston for several years and who was virtually unhittable during Boston's 2013 championship run.

Foulke threw an 84 mph fastball outside for ball two, with Sierra smartly laying off. The next pitch was virtually identical, again just missing off the outside corner, bringing the count to 3–1. Foulke was not giving Sierra anything to hit, staying away, away, away.

The fifth pitch of the at-bat was a change that missed low and away, and Sierra took the free pass, his fifth straight time reaching base on the night. And so with two out and Sierra at first, Tony Clark stepped to the plate.

Francona paced the dugout, his cheeks full, chomping on his chewing tobacco. It was a habit he'd had for years. He tried to quit several times, and once in 2007, he even bet Red Sox president Larry Lucchino $20,000 (to be donated to Boston's Dana-Farber Cancer Institute) that he could quit during the season. In 2016, as manager of the Cleveland Indians, his habit cost him a tooth.

"Right before the game, I mean, like literally, my lower tooth, the veneer popped out while I was chewing. That thing came off, and I'm chewing, and it felt crunchy. I was like, 'Uh-oh.' So I undid my tobacco, and there's my tooth." So he called James Quinlan, then the head athletic trainer for the Indians. "I'm pissed now," Francona recalled. "I called James down and I gave him my tooth and I said, 'You call [the team dentist] and tell him I'm going to beat him.' I said, 'Tell [him] he better find me a [expletive] dentist up here tomorrow.' So then James comes back in like the third inning and I said, 'Tell me you found a dentist.' He goes, 'I came to tell you about Trevor [Bauer, Cleveland's starting pitcher who had injured his hand].' I go, 'Screw Trevor!'"

Francona managed with a cool style, trusting his players to perform to the best of their abilities. He was easygoing, and he managed to keep clubhouse drama in-house. In 2005, he felt severe chest pains that, along with a life-threatening pulmonary embolism he suffered in 2002, led to circulation problems. Francona routinely—even on hot summer days—wore a top over his uniform jersey to aid in circulation.

He had great confidence in Foulke, who had been brought over from Oakland in the off-season, filling a major hole in the Red Sox' roster. Foulke had earned every bit of that trust, both from a terrific regular season and his postseason work to this point. After 2.2 innings of scoreless relief the night before, he was back on the mound, trying to keep the powerful Yankees off the scoreboard.

"I can see now what Terry Francona meant when he said that he hadn't slept since spring training," Sutcliffe joked. "He's had a lot of tough decisions to make. First of all to get Boston to the playoffs, and now to keep them there."

Foulke's first pitch was a changeup that drifted well off the plate for ball one. Clark was having a miserable night at the plate with a fly out, ground out, and two strikeouts; but one mistake by Foulke could put Boston right back in a hole.

"Clark tonight is 0 for 4, but he can be a very dangerous hitter," O'Brien said. "If you groove one, he can hit it four hundred and fifty feet."

Foulke threw a fastball on the farthest reaches of the outside corner that Kellogg called a strike. Foulke benefitted from a generous strike zone on that side of the plate from Kellogg. Clark, not one to complain, shook his head gently, about as much of a protest as he would ever offer.

Foulke again dotted the outside corner with a fastball, and Clark was suddenly down 1–2 in the count. Foulke was one strike away from getting Boston to the bottom of the ninth tied, with the top of the lineup due up.

"I would check Sierra," Sutcliffe said on MLB. "He doesn't run like he used to, but he can still run. We saw on the infield single he legged out. Make him shorten up. Make sure that he's aware that you know he's there, that's all."

Instead of coming home, Foulke did as Sutcliffe suggested, throwing to first to chase Sierra back to the bag. Sierra would be off at the crack of the bat, and any extra base hit, if he got a good jump, could be enough to score him from first.

Sutcliffe then said Foulke should focus on the hitter and maybe throw a fastball, but, he said, "You've gotta have enough gas to get it by him. How does Keith Foulke's arm feel?"

When Foulke finally came to the plate, he decided to throw inside, something he hadn't done in two batters. It was a typical Foulke fastball, no more than 85 miles an hour, and Clark turned on it, ripping it down the right field line and deep. It headed for the corner stands but didn't quite have home run distance.

On MLB, O'Brien made the call: "Fly ball, hooked to the corner, by the Pesky Pole…that is a fair ball, up into the crowd! It'll be an automatic double, and Rubén Sierra has to stop at third base. The Yankees can't score on that because it bounced up into the crowd, and a very lucky hop for the Boston Red Sox."

"They catch a huge break here," said Sutcliffe, "as Sierra had a good jump."

Mike Cole, reliving the game for NESN in May 2020, called this the "luckiest break in franchise history."

Boston Globe writer Chad Finn recalled, "I've watched it five times in the last few minutes, and I still have no idea how Tony Clark's ground-rule double with a runner on in the top of the ninth off Keith Foulke did not stay in play. To that point, it might have been the most fortuitous bounce the Red Sox have ever received."

Until that point, every bounce had always seemed to go New York's way. In the 2000s, Boston has, up through the completion of the 2019 season, won four World Series titles, more than any other team. Along with the success of the Patriots (six Super Bowl victories), Celtics (one NBA championship), and Bruins (one Stanley Cup), fans outside New England under the age of, say, twenty-five think that Boston is the luckiest sports city ever, getting fortunate break after beneficial call after favorable bounce, one after the other.

But what they don't know—because they have never experienced it—is the utter futility that Boston franchises experienced. The Patriots lived for years as the worst team in the NFL. The Red Sox could never get past the Yankees, and even when they had the World Series in their grasp, they fumbled it away (see Game 6, 1986 World Series). The Bruins hadn't won since the early '70s. The Celtics—the NBA's greatest dynasty—hadn't won since 1986. Things hadn't gone Boston's way in decades, and for the Red Sox, for 86 seasons. To receive a break like this was almost impossible to fathom for any Red Sox fan at the time.

Lucky as it was, Foulke still had to get another out, and New York had runners at second and third. One more hit, or an error, or a passed ball, would give the Yankees the lead with Rivera waiting to close it out.

"We said last night kiddingly," McCarver reminded viewers, "baseball is a game of inch." Singular. "That ball stays in the ballpark, Sierra scores rather easily."

Foulke missed with a ball to Cairo, the next hitter, and then threw an 83 mph "fastball"—roughly the equivalent of a decent high-school pitcher's velocity—down the middle, belt-high, that Cairo popped up to first. Mientkiewicz calmly settled under it in foul territory and squeezed it for the final out. Foulke escaped, his arm on fumes, with Mientkiewicz recording all three putouts in the inning.

IN THE BOTTOM of the inning, Rivera had to deal with Boston's 1-2-3 hitters, Damon, Cabrera, and Ramirez, with Ortiz lurking after that. He had "blown" the save the inning before, yet retired all three hitters he had faced, on 11 pitches. The statistic implied that Rivera did not do his job, but it's tough to ask any pitcher to do more than he did in the previous inning.

In between innings, three Boston starting pitchers made their way to the Boston bullpen: Tim Wakefield, Derek Lowe, and Curt Schilling. Schilling in particular was a curious move, given that he was the presumptive Game 6 starter. Francona presumably felt that there's no Game 6 if you can't win Game 5, but it was unclear still how Schilling's ankle would hold up. Uncertainty notwithstanding, the sight of him heading to the bullpen just in case caused a stir in Fenway and in the FOX broadcast booth.

Damon was up first, having a horrific game and series, with just one hit in his first 22 at-bats. Rivera, coming off a two-inning, 40-pitch outing the night before, needed to be economical. He pumped one of his legendary cut fastballs in for a strike to start the at-bat. His next pitch missed low and inside, and then he threw the same pitch that Damon couldn't lay off this time. He unsuccessfully checked his swing and missed for strike two. On the 1–2 pitch, Damon shattered his bat, sending splinters out toward the mound. The ball went up the middle slowly. Cairo hustled over, gloved it, and threw to first, but the speedy Damon beat it out easily for an infield hit to start the inning.

"'It went down a hero' is what's said in the dugout when you break a bat and you get a base hit with it," said Sutcliffe amidst the din of 35,000 screaming fans. "Now some decisions to make. You gotta make it happen if you're Terry Francona right now. You have to. Keith Foulke is done. You don't want to use Schilling. You don't want to use Wakefield. You don't want to use Derek Lowe. You want to end it right now."

In the eleventh inning of Game 4, Damon had gotten on base and stole second off Tom Gordon on an 0–1 count. Cabrera couldn't drive him in, but if there was any man besides Dave Roberts that Boston could have on first with nobody out, it was Damon. He had stolen only 19 bases against 8 caught stealing in 2004, but typically he was an excellent base thief. From 2002 to 2003, he stole 61 times and was caught just 12. In the 2004 post-season up to this point, he was successful in all four of his stolen base attempts.

For his part, Jorge Posada had a quick release but an average to below-average arm behind the plate. In 2004, he threw out 27 percent of would-be base stealers, compared to the league average of 32 percent. For his career, he threw out a lower percentage than his peers.

Rivera tossed to first to keep an eye on Damon. New York positioned its infield, expecting a bunt, but that wasn't the only card Francona could play. He could sacrifice with a good bat-handler in Cabrera and a speedster at first in Damon. He could call a straight steal for Damon. Or he could hit-and-run, sending Damon while having Cabrera hit away. That's what Boston did when Nixon singled in the eighth to advance Roberts to third.

Damon took off with Rivera's first movement, and Cabrera squared to bunt. Rivera threw a hard fastball high and tight, and Cabrera pulled back his bat. Posada popped out of his crouch, caught the pitch, and fired an absolute laser to Jeter covering second. The Yankee captain caught it and, in one very smooth motion, snapped a tag onto Damon's foot just a split second before he reached second.

"What a throw by Posada on a tough pitch, up and in to Cabrera," said McCarver, a former catcher who understood the value of good defensive play behind the plate. "I mean, a bullet to second base, and a quick tag by Jeter."

On the 2–1 pitch, now with nobody on base, Cabrera hit a routine grounder to shortstop, and Jeter made easy work of it for the second out. Suddenly, an inning that seemed so promising was on the verge of coming up empty.

But Boston still had Ramirez up, and he could end the game with one mighty swing of his bat. Rivera wasn't finished yet. Ramirez was 2–4 with two singles, but what Boston needed was a home run. Rivera's first pitch missed a little high for ball one.

Leiter noted that Rivera had never pitched in back-to-back games where he went two or more innings in his career. He had thrown two in Game 4 and needed one more out to complete his second inning here in Game 5. Like Foulke, he had been used a lot, and there was a reason why Torre was hesitant to use him to start the eighth.

Rivera bore a fastball in on Manny's hands. Ramirez spun out of the way, and it looked like he swung. Kellogg called it a ball, not seeing Ramirez' swing, but Posada quickly appealed to Joe West at first. West held his hands out in a "safe" sign, indicating no swing, and the Yankees nearly went ballistic. Replay showed that Ramirez clearly went around.

"Joe Torre can't believe it, and I can't either," O'Brien said.

"Look at Posada! Look at Posada and Rivera! Look at the Yankee dugout! Oh my goodness gracious," said a disbelieving Trupiano. "Everybody in North America thought that Manny swung at that pitch, except Joe West."

"Huge difference between a 1–1 count and a 2–0 count that Joe West just handed Manny Ramirez," said Sutcliffe.

For his career, Ramirez was an excellent hitter in either count. He would bat .410 with a 1.178 OPS on a 1–1 count and .428 with a 1.308 OPS on a 2–0 count. Either way he was terrific, but he was nonetheless better—like most hitters are—on a 2–0 count.

Rivera delivered, and Ramirez lofted a fly ball to fairly deep center. The crowd rose for a moment but then realized that it would stay in the park. Williams made short work of the routine fly, and the side was retired.

For the second straight game, the Yankees and Red Sox were going to extra innings, tied at four.

10

THE TENTH INNING

Bronson Arroyo replaced Keith Foulke to start the tenth, and, like Boston had in the ninth, New York had the top of their lineup coming to bat. The Yankees had knocked him around terribly in Game 3, pounding him for six runs on six hits in just two innings. Of the 13 New York batters Arroyo faced that night, two homered (Matsui and A-Rod), three doubled (Matsui, A-Rod, and Sierra), one singled (Williams), two walked (Jeter, Sheffield), and five were retired (one on a double-play ball). His early exit forced the Red Sox to use five relievers, who threw a combined 155 pitches over seven innings. By any measure, his Game 3 start was a disaster, and it put the Red Sox in a 3–0 hole in the series. At this point, however, Boston manager Terry Francona had few good options.

The advent of the modern closer meant, among other things, that managers would often hold them back for a "save" situation. That is, many closers are uncomfortable entering a game either behind or when the game is tied, and so managers often only put them in when their team is ahead and the score is within three runs. And sometimes the result is that their closer—theoretically their best relief pitcher—never sees the game.

A classic case of this occurred on October 4, 2016, in the AL Wild Card playoff game between Toronto and Baltimore. Oriole starter Chris Tillman lasted just 4.1 innings in the game, allowing two runs. From that point through the eleventh inning, Baltimore used six other pitchers as the game stretched past the normal nine innings. As inning after inning went by, Baltimore manager Buck Showalter had the option of using his best reliever, closer Zach Britton, who had been spectacular that season, posting a 0.54 ERA, 0.84 WHIP, and 9.9 k/9. He actually warmed up in the eighth inning but never got in the game.

Jay Jaffe wrote in his game report for *Sports Illustrated*, "The AL wild-card game was a thriller, won by the Blue Jays 5–2 in 11 innings via Edwin Encarnacion's walk-off three-run homer. Had the blast been off of closer Zach Britton, the Orioles could say that they lost with their best, but curiously, Britton—who had warmed up in the eighth inning—wasn't in the game. Ubaldo Jimenez, who finished the season with a 5.44 ERA, was."

This wasn't the first time a manager made such a miscalculation. In Game 4 of the 2003 World Series, Yankee manager Joe Torre let Jeff Weaver pitch the eleventh inning against the Marlins instead of going to his best reliever, Rivera. Weaver did the job in the eleventh but then allowed a walk-off home run by

Álex González in the twelfth to give the Marlins the win. Rivera never left the bullpen.

Jaffe wrote, "Buck Showalter's decision not to use Britton was even more extreme than both [New York in 2003 and a similar move by Atlanta in 2013], as it came in a sudden death situation in what was already a do-or-die game. It will go down as one of the biggest managerial blunders in postseason history."

Why was it a blunder? Well, simply put, you can't save your best reliever for a situation that may never come, *especially* in a playoff game, and especially in a loser-goes-home game. Using lesser relievers in key late innings or extra innings gives the other team a better chance to score, and thus you never get the save opportunity you're saving your closer for.

It burned Joe Torre in 2003, and it burned Buck Showalter in 2016. It did not burn Terry Francona in 2004, however, because he employed a different strategy. He used his best relievers right away, even in a non-save situation, to keep the score close and give his team a chance to win the game. His second-best reliever, Mike Timlin, had come in in the seventh, and then Keith Foulke, his best reliever, entered in the eighth and pitched through the ninth. Francona used his best relievers first, hoping to extend the game, and if the game went longer, then he figured he could use his lesser relievers.

Torre did the same thing, of course, although his decision-making still fit the traditional closer model. After Mussina, he went to Sturtze and then his two best relievers, Gordon and Rivera. With the game tied in the tenth, however, he too would have to go with lesser pitchers. But in both cases, Francona and Torre emptied their bullpens with their better pitchers first and then figured the rest out later.

Arroyo had been a solid pitcher for Boston in 2004, going 10–9 with a 4.03 ERA. His high leg kick was unique in the game, and he had a phenomenal sweeping curve that came almost sidearm, to go along with a modest fastball. He had won Game 3 of the ALDS against Anaheim, pitching six terrific innings, allowing just three hits and two runs. His fortunes changed facing the Bronx Bombers in Fenway; but Francona, after using Timlin and Foulke already, turned to Arroyo for the tenth.

"Look at whose hands this ball game has been handed to," Sutcliffe said. "You've got Bronson Arroyo, you've got [Félix] Heredia up in the bullpen. Not what either manager had envisioned."

Arroyo threw a sinking change over the inside corner for strike one against Jeter, who had the huge hit in the sixth to give New York the lead. On the next pitch, he fired a fastball, this one on the outside corner, that Jeter, who may have been looking for the curve, took for strike two. Just like that, Arroyo was up 0–2 in the count. Jeter stepped out and took a slow walk, collecting his thoughts and refocusing. This is where Arroyo was likely to snap off one of his electric curveballs.

"Let's see if he [Arroyo] can handle that adrenaline right now. He's got the count where he wants it. He'd like to get this breaking ball on the outer half of the plate or beyond," Sutcliffe mused.

He indeed did throw the curve, but it was a bad one. It hung thigh-high, dead center of the plate. Jeter swung and fouled it back and out of play. He missed a good pitch to hit, and Arroyo got away with a mistake.

"Jeter knocks it into the stands," O'Brien said.

"He should have knocked it into the stands," Sutcliffe replied. "But I'm talking about the stands above the Green Monster."

Arroyo then dipped down to the side and sent a wicked curve way outside that Jeter watched go by for a ball to make the count

1–2. Jeter almost called time but settled back in as Arroyo delivered the 1–2 pitch. He took something off it and threw a slower curve that Jeter was way out in front of and popped up to short, an easy catch for Cabrera for the first out. Upon entering the Yankee dugout, Jeter let out a loud f-bomb. He knew he missed a golden opportunity on the 0–2 pitch.

Rodriguez was next. The last time he faced Arroyo, he hit a home run to lead off the third inning of Game 3 that tied the game at four. New York would never look back after that. A-Rod had been on base three times thus far in the game, with two walks and a hit-by-pitch. He also had missed a great chance to drive in a huge run in the eighth inning when Timlin struck him out with Cairo at third and only one out.

Arroyo's first pitch was a 91 mph fastball that he blew by Rodriguez for strike one. Following the same pattern as he did with Jeter, he pumped a fastball on the outside corner but just missed for a ball. Then he missed inside with another fastball, giving Rodriguez a favorable 2–1 count. He tried to go upstairs but only got 87 mph on the pitch, but it was elevated enough that Rodriguez fouled it straight back. Another pitch that Arroyo was fortunate to get away with.

Once again, he dipped down to the side and sent a spinner way off the plate that brought the count full. The crowd, tense, rose and clapped for the twenty-seven-year-old pitcher. Rodriguez, expecting a curve, swung and missed at a 90 mph sinking fastball on the inner half of the plate for strike three. New York had been looking curve, and Arroyo was killing them with modest fastballs in good locations.

"He just came right at him," said Sutcliffe. "This was all he could get on a fastball, 90 miles an hour. Forget the breaking ball,

I don't have the feel for it right now, but I'm feeling pretty good about myself after this."

That brought up Sheffield. For Red Sox fans, Sheffield was one of the most frightening hitters in all of baseball. He exuded power. His upright stance and strong bat waggle made it feel like he was going to crush every single pitch 450 feet. "Who's your dealer?" Boston fans chanted, referring to Sheffield's involvement with BALCO.

Arroyo started Sheffield off with a soft curve that nipped the outside corner. Another curve, way off the plate, evened the count. The 1–1 pitch was a 12-6 soft curve that missed high, though not by much.

On the 2–1 pitch, Arroyo made another mistake. He dipped to the side a little more and hung a slider. It just spun a little above the belt, and Sheffield took a wicked cut, connecting, and ripping it foul against the left field facade. A very hard strike, but a strike nonetheless. That was a reminder of why Arroyo had to be so careful with Sheffield. He had incredibly fast hands and could turn on just about any pitch at any moment. Buck said, "If you're Terry Francona, you have no idea what to expect from a guy like Arroyo coming out of the bullpen. One day of rest, with memories of that start on Saturday night, your team facing elimination, you're dealing with the top of the lineup, and Arroyo so far, so good."

With the count even at two balls, two strikes, Arroyo barely missed inside with a slider to once again bring the count full. On the 3–2, he dipped to the side again and threw a hard slider that Sheffield swung at and missed, spinning himself around in the batter's box.

O'Brien's call: "Swing and a miss on the changeup! He struck him out! The Red Sox bullpen has been brilliant the last couple of nights, allowing just one run in ten and two-thirds innings!"

Arroyo had gotten the 1-2-3 hitters in the Yankee lineup in order, including consecutive strikeouts of two of the game's best hitters, Rodriguez and Sheffield.

JOE TORRE SUMMONED twenty-nine-year-old southpaw Félix Heredia to start the tenth, and the reason for that was obvious. He was a sidewinding left-hander, and Boston had David Ortiz and Doug Mientkiewicz due up. Heredia had debuted in 1996 as a twenty-one-year-old with the Florida Marlins organization, pitching 16.2 innings. In 1997, he was a key part of the Marlins' bullpen, pitching 56.2 innings with a 4.29 ERA in 56 games for a World Series champion team. He had never been great, but at this point, he was expected to do one job: get left-handed hitters out in the latter innings of close baseball games. Over his ten-year career, right-handed batters hit .279 with a .374 OBP and a .799 OPS against the Dominican hurler. But left-handed batters hit just .221 with a .303 OBP and .677 OPS—a considerable difference. In 2004, the gap was significantly wider. Righties hit .333 with a .400 OBP and .900 OPS, while lefties hit just .216 with a .326 OBP and .731 OPS.

From Boston's point of view, the call for Heredia was equally obvious. David Ortiz in 2004 hit .326 with a 1.082 OPS against right-handed pitchers, but a notably lower, yet still respectable, .250 with a .784 OPS against lefties. Mientkiewicz' splits weren't nearly as large (.246 avg. vs. righties, .220 vs. lefties), but still, pitchers like Heredia were made for this moment.

Heredia had a strange Yankee playoff debut against the Twins in Game 3 of the ALDS. He was called upon in the bottom of the eighth inning with an 8–1 lead to face left-handed slugger Justin Morneau. He retired him on a groundout and then came back out in the bottom of the ninth. He promptly hit two straight batters before Torre pulled him. He hadn't pitched since then but now was called on to take out Boston's biggest bat, David Ortiz.

The crowd smelled blood, knowing the drop-off from Rivera to Heredia was enormous. Heredia's first pitch was a slider slung from a three-quarter angle that dipped low and away for ball one. A very close pitch that did not go Heredia's way. Heredia was one year older than Ortiz, and the two were born in cities just 70 miles apart as the crow flies but 114 miles and three hours away by car along routes 44 and 2 on the southern side of the island.

Heredia threw a fastball at 88 mph on the outside corner and was fouled off by Ortiz, evening the count. Paul Quantrill, the losing pitcher in Game 4, was loosening in the Yankee bullpen. Heredia's next pitch was a fastball inside, causing Ortiz to jack-knife out of the way. At 2–1, he had a favorable count. Heredia had walked nine batters in 14 career postseason innings, and he could ill afford to go 3–1 to Big Papi.

Heredia wasn't as good as Ortiz, but he wasn't in the majors for no reason. He had a competitor's spirit, and he challenged Ortiz on the next pitch, blowing a fastball by him to even the count. Ortiz on the swing was trying to end the game right then, right there, but came up empty.

On the 2–2, Heredia threw a slider in the dirt, and Ortiz chased, but checked his swing. Posada immediately appealed and Jeff Nelson, the third base umpire, quickly rang up Ortiz, who couldn't believe it and argued the call. The crowd exploded in epithets at Nelson. Playoff intensity indeed.

"It was close," McCarver said, viewing the FOX replay. "It did not look like he went around."

Sutcliffe on MLB disagreed. "That's right there on that line. To me, that is a swing."

Boston's best bat was out, and Mientkiewicz came up for his first at-bat of the game. Heredia started him off with a fastball inside for ball one and threw the exact same pitch with the exact same result to make it 2–0. In the Boston dugout, Ortiz sat simmering, hoping that hadn't been his last chance of the night.

As Posada ran out to talk to Heredia, Sutcliffe related an interesting story about Mientkiewicz. "I think he's responsible for one of the best quotes I've ever heard from a current baseball player. He hit .414 for the Olympic team a few years ago [the 2000 US team—the only one of seven teams to win the Gold Medal for the United States in its national pastime game in the Olympics]. But he was quoted as saying, 'No one's ever gonna remember what I hit. They're gonna remember that we won.' And I think when he put this uniform on [Boston], and Cabrera put it on, and Dave Roberts put it on, they became a 'we.'"

Heredia missed again with yet another fastball, this one almost hitting him. Up 3–0, Mientkiewicz would either be taking all the way or have the green light to try to end it if he got something he liked. The Yankee lefty threw a great pitch on the outside corner at the knees, a pitch that Mientkiewicz wanted no part of. Strike one.

Sutcliffe said, "He's gonna get exactly the same pitch here now. I mean, you just lock in…You lock in, you think right now fastball middle-in. A little bit up. If it's anything but, you let it go."

The pitch was precisely what Sutcliffe said Mientkiewicz should be looking for, an 83 mph fastball on the inner half above the belt. He took a huge cut but only managed to foul it off. From 3–0, the count was now full.

Heredia drilled a fastball low and inside, close enough for Mientkiewicz to have to swing, and he spoiled it, fouling it off to the left to stay alive.

"Mientkiewicz, more of a line-drive hitter," Trupiano said on the radio. "Doesn't hit a lot of home runs. Has occasional power." He spoiled another couple of pitches, making Heredia work. Two of them might have been ball four but were too close for any batter in Mientkiewicz' position to gamble, as no hitter wants to get caught looking.

"He has cracked three balls out of Fenway Park," McCarver deadpanned. "Foul, of course."

On the ninth pitch of the at-bat, Heredia threw a slider that caught too much of the plate. Mientkiewicz ripped a liner to deep right. Sheffield took a step in, realized he misjudged it, got spun around and gave a futile chase for the ball, which rocketed over his head, took a big hop on the warning track, and bounced into the stands for an automatic double. Once again, Boston had the winning run in scoring position, and Joe Torre came out to call for Quantrill.

"Well, that ball should have been caught," Castiglione said. "It was hit very hard, a fastball right down the middle, Mientkiewicz really cranked it, but Sheffield misjudged it. The same Sheffield who has a big quote in today's *Boston Herald*, calling the Red Sox a 'walking disaster.'"

Heredia grew up south of the United States, but Quantrill came from the north. Born in London, Ontario, he was drafted in 1986 by the Dodgers as a high school player, but he didn't sign, choosing instead to play baseball at the University of Wisconsin. In 1989, the Red Sox drafted him in the sixth round, and three years later, at age twenty-three, he made his major league debut. He had a terrific rookie year for Boston in 1992, pitching in 27 games, compiling a stellar 2.19 ERA. Known primarily as a ground ball pitcher, he spent two and a half seasons in Boston before being traded to the Phillies. Philadelphia turned him into a starter in 1995, and in 33 appearances, he struggled. The next year he was in Toronto, after having been traded for Howard Battle and Rico Jordan, and started 20 games before being moved to the bullpen. He spent five years with the Blue Jays, recording several outstanding seasons from 1997 to 2001 (3.05 ERA over that span). After being traded in the off-season to the Los Angeles Dodgers for Luke Prokopec and minor leaguer Chad Ricketts, he pitched even better for the Dodgers in 2002 and 2003, leading the league in appearances and posting a combined 2.22 ERA.

New York signed him before the 2004 season, and he quickly became one of Torre's favorite arms out of the Yankee bullpen. He led not only New York in appearances but all of MLB as well, pitching in 86 games, just three short of the major league single-season record. His effectiveness dropped off considerably, however, from his time in LA, as his ERA in New York ballooned to 4.72. Overuse may have caught up with him. He was solid for the first 64 games, with an ERA of 3.00; but in the last 22 games of the season, he pitched 20.1 innings, allowing 44 hits, nine walks, and 26 runs, pitching to a ghastly 11.07 ERA and 2.61 WHIP. His last 11 games in particular were even worse: a 13.50 ERA and a 2.80 WHIP.

He had been better in the playoffs in the first three appearances of the postseason, however, with no runs and four hits allowed in 3.2 innings. But in Game 4, he allowed the walk-off home run by David Ortiz in the twelfth inning that kept Boston's hopes alive. He was being called upon to strand Mientkiewicz and keep Boston from winning Game 5.

Gabe Kapler, who pinch-ran earlier in the game, was playing right field in place of Trot Nixon. If Nixon had been in, Torre likely would have stuck with Heredia, but with the right-handed Kapler up, Quantrill got the call. In his early twenties, Kapler had a fairly potent bat. From 1999 to 2001 with the Tigers and Rangers, he hit .272 with 49 home runs in 1,343 at-bats, a rate of 21 homers per 162 games. Not a slugger, but a guy who had the ability to put one out of the park.

His power waned, however, since the 2001 season, and from 2002 to 2004, he hit just 12 homers over 830 at-bats. But he also had a .275 average over that span, and all Boston needed was a hit, not a home run. Quantrill had work to do.

Fenway rocked as fans clapped in unison as Quantrill finished his warm-up pitches and Kapler stepped into the box. Quantrill's first pitch was a slider that missed outside for ball one. Best-selling author and Red Sox superfan Stephen King looked on anxiously. After a bluff to second to keep Mientkiewicz honest, he fired a fastball high and away for ball two. A hitter's count for Kapler. Quantrill threw a poor pitch, a fastball meant to be low and away but it rode up and in, but Kapler could only ground it weakly to second. Cairo fielded it cleanly for the out, moving Mientkiewicz to third. Ninety feet away from victory.

"Oh, here's their guy," Sutcliffe said of the next hitter, Jason Varitek. "The heart and soul, to a man, the Boston Red Sox will tell you, for their team, is at home plate right now."

Varitek had good numbers against Quantrill over his career— 6–17 (.353). Boston needed a hit to get Mientkiewicz in. A hit or an error or any pitch that got by Posada. A wild pitch was unlikely, as Quantrill had thrown only five in his entire fourteen-year career spanning more than 5,400 batters faced.

Posada went out to talk to Quantrill about how to handle Varitek. Bill Mueller was on deck, and it was not likely they would walk Varitek. Quantrill started Varitek off with a fastball that missed outside. Varitek's last at-bat had been the sacrifice fly that tied the game in the eighth, and now he had an opportunity to drive in the winning run. A sinker from Quantrill missed low, and now Varitek was in the driver's seat at 2–0. An antsy Fenway crowd hoped for a hit.

Quantrill delivered another sinker that missed Posada's intended target (low and away) but managed to pick up the inside corner for a strike. On the 2–1, Varitek hit a sky-high pop-up behind third. Matsui raced in from left, Rodriguez from third, but it was Jeter who ranged over from shortstop to make the catch and end the inning. Another threat yielded no runs, and the two teams headed to the eleventh inning, still tied at four.

11

THE ELEVENTH INNING

In the top of the eleventh, Terry Francona worked from the same playbook as Torre had used against Ortiz and Mientkiewicz the prior inning. He brought in sidewinding lefty Mike Myers to face Hideki Matsui. It was an interesting move. In the top of the tenth, Bronson Arroyo had made quick work of the Yankees and, being a starting pitcher, had the ability to go multiple innings. In a long and protracted game, that could have been useful. But managers in the playoffs typically don't assume games will go deep into extra innings. The game could be won or lost *this* inning, and so they typically do whatever they can to get the outs they need right now.

"Hideki Matsui will be first up for the Yankees here in the eleventh inning," Joe Buck said. "A 4–4 game, and Matsui, who has had an incredible ALCS, will deal with Mike Myers." Matsui had one hit—a single way back in the third—but nothing since. For Myers, this was his third appearance of the series, with his first two being unsuccessful. In Game 3, as the game got out of hand, Myers was called on to pitch two innings to save a beleaguered bullpen. In those two innings, he allowed five hits (including four in a row at one point) and a two-run homer to none other than Matsui, a left-handed hitter Myers is paid to specifically get out. With two on and one out in the ninth, he escaped further damage when Tony Clark hit a bullet, lining into a double play. In Game 4, the Yankees had a threat going in the eleventh, as Alan Embree gave up a single to Cairo, a sacrifice to Jeter, and then an intentional walk to Sheffield. Myers was called on to get Matsui, and he promptly walked him on four straight pitches, loading the bases. Francona took him out and brought in Curtis Leskanic, who got Bernie Williams to fly out to center to end the threat.

But Francona chose Myers over Arroyo anyway, and in some ways this was a sign that Boston's fortunes were changing. Pre-2004, this move likely would have backfired. The "Curse of the Bambino," a phrase indicating Boston's decades of futility and bad luck following their infamous trade of Babe Ruth to the Yankees, would have suggested that Myers would have given up a double or worse, and the usually negative and surly Boston sports media would have second-guessed Francona forever, asking why he would even dream of removing an effective pitcher for one who had previously struggled just because "the book" says so.

Myers, who threw almost submarine-style, stared in as Matsui stepped into the batter's box. Over his career, Myers' splits were dramatic. Righties pounded him to the tune of a .301 average,

.400 OBP, and .878 OPS. However, lefties only hit .219 against him with a .304 OBP and .635 OPS. "The book" made statistical sense, but Francona also had to manage by his wits. He believed this was the right move.

Myers' first pitch was a slider at the knees for strike one. His release angle was so extreme, it made for a very uncomfortable at-bat for most left-handed hitters. Alan Embree, another lefty, was warming in the pen, but he had a more conventional three-quarter to overhand delivery that left-handed hitters could handle more easily.

Myers' second pitch was another slider, his bread and butter, that rode away from Matsui past the outside corner of the plate. Matsui swung and missed and, just like that, he was down 0–2. Now a typical move for a lefty here would be to get Matsui to chase something out of the strike zone, and in this kind of matchup, that usually meant a slider down and away off the plate. A sidewinding lefty would look to start it over the plate to look like a strike, but the idea was for it to move enough so that by the time Matsui swung, the ball was long out of reach.

Instead, Myers went with a fastball and tried to get Matsui to chase that out of the strike zone. It missed high, and Matsui, possibly thinking Myers would throw the slider, let it go for a ball.

Sutcliffe, so insightful to the thinking of pitchers, said, "Myers has been around a long time, and he's kind of gotten himself into a pattern with that 0–2 pitch, that high fastball there we've seen a lot. And then he usually tries to follow it up with a breaking ball off the plate, to get you to chase it. Look breaking ball, if you're Matsui, if it starts out at you, it's a pitch you can hit."

Myers did exactly as Sutcliffe predicted, throwing a slider that started over the plate and moved away from Matsui, who couldn't lay off it. He struck out. Francona's move paid off, and he promptly walked to the mound to get the ball from his left-handed specialist, patting him on the back and calling for Embree, who was better equipped to deal with the Yankee switch-hitters due up next, all of whom would be hitting from the right side.

Like most of Boston's relief corps, Embree was a true veteran, now pitching in his eleventh season (he would pitch 16 total for his career); and at the age of 34, the native of The Dalles, Oregon, who was drafted out of high school by Cleveland in 1989, had proved to be a valuable member of Boston's bullpen. After pitching for Cleveland for three years, he was traded along with Kenny Lofton to Atlanta for Marquis Grissom and David Justice, then was traded in 1998 to Arizona for Russ Springer, and then in the off-season in 1998 to San Francisco for Dante Powell. In 2001, the Giants traded him to the White Sox for minor leaguer Derek Hasselhoff and cash. He was granted free agency in the off-season and signed with San Diego. In June of the 2002 season, the Padres traded him, along with minor leaguer Andy Shibilo, to the Red Sox for Dan Giese and minor leaguer Brad Baker. Embree's path to Boston was indeed a long and winding road.

In his younger years, he could dial his fastball up to 98 miles an hour, but by the time he got to Boston, he typically threw in the low 90s, hoping that the reduced velocity would lessen the strain on his arm. He accompanied his good fastball with a sharp slider, a potent two-pitch mix. In an oddity of baseball line scores, five years after his appearance in Game 5 in 2004, on July 7, 2009, he would be awarded a win without throwing a single pitch. Pitching for the Colorado Rockies in his last year, he came into the game and faced one batter but promptly picked Austin Kearns of Cincinnati off first base, ending the eighth inning. Colorado would score in the bottom of the eighth, and Colorado closer Huston Street earned the save in the ninth, giving Embree the win.

Embree had extensive postseason experience prior to 2004. From 1995 to 2003, he appeared in 19 playoff games, pitching 14 innings, allowing just six hits, three walks, and two runs, for a sparkling 1.29 ERA and 0.64 WHIP. In 2003, he pitched in five games in the ALCS against New York and had a 0.00 ERA and 0.64 WHIP in 4.2 innings. In 2004, his entire playoff run was excellent, giving Boston 7.1 innings and allowing just two runs. This was Game 5 of the ALCS, though, and he had pitched in all four previous league championship series games. In those four games, he allowed eight hits and two runs, so the ALCS ride had been a little bumpy. But he was a solid professional, and Francona had great confidence in him whether he was facing left- or right-handed hitters.

Bernie Williams stepped in and, on an 0–1 pitch, hit a letter-high 92 mph fastball into the air, and it fell to the grass in right center between Damon and Kapler for a base hit.

Posada, another switch-hitter batting right-handed against Embree, was next. In his younger days, Williams was a decent base-stealing threat, stealing 15 or more bases four times between 1994 and 1998. But in 2004, he only tried to steal six times and had been caught five of them. Embree had to keep an eye on him but wasn't worried about Williams running.

Embree's first pitch to Posada was a fastball for a strike at 89 miles an hour, about 3 to 4 mph slower than his usual velocity. If he couldn't run it up there as fast as he normally could, it would mean Embree's control and slider needed to be better. His second pitch was a 91 mph fastball low and away that Posada fouled off into the seats. At 0–2, Embree had options now. He eschewed the slider and poured a 92 mph fastball down and in that Posada swung out and missed.

"Most swinging strikeouts by major league hitters are on balls out of the strike zone," McCarver said. "That one, no exception."

Rubén Sierra, the third of four straight switch-hitters (Tony Clark would be the fourth, due up next), stepped in. Embree missed with a fastball and then threw a nasty sinking fastball that Sierra swung on and missed to even the count at 1–1. Embree, chewing on his tobacco, concentrated on ending the inning. The last time Embree faced Sierra was the previous night, and Sierra got the best of him with a single. Sierra fouled the next one back, and Embree had a good pitcher's count at one ball, two strikes. The crowd stood to its feet and, in full throat, urged Embree on. He fired a fastball above the letters, and Sierra couldn't lay off. He swung and missed to strike out. The last five Yankee outs had been via the strikeout, all swinging. Francona was pulling all the right strings.

IN THE BOTTOM of the inning, Paul Quantrill returned to the mound after his successful tenth inning. Bill Mueller was first up, and Quantrill delivered a first-pitch strike. Always good to get ahead in the count. On the second pitch, Quantrill jammed him, and Mueller lofted a high pop into shallow right. Cairo raced out, Sheffield came in, but thinking that Cairo had a bead on it, Sheffield slowed a little. Cairo reached up, but the ball fell harmlessly between them for a soft leadoff single. Mueller took a wide turn around first, and Sheffield picked up the ball with his bare hand and fired back to Clark, but Mueller dove back safely. He jammed his left ring finger diving back to the bag and grimaced in pain. Baseball is a strange game. Sometimes you hit bullets that turn into outs (Bellhorn earlier in the game), and sometimes you hit weak flares that fall in for hits.

Now Francona faced the classic question of whether or not to bunt. He had his 9 hitter up in Bellhorn, who had been having a miserable series but who had taken terrific swings all game. On deck was Damon, who also had been having a disastrous series himself. A successful sacrifice would put Mueller in scoring position, with Boston needing one hit from either Damon or Cabrera to win the game. But the tradeoff was that it would cost an out.

"He's gonna bunt," Sutcliffe predicted. "But you gotta get a pitch you can handle. Again, the pitcher is the man that's in trouble. I didn't do a lot of hitting at the big-league level, but I did do a lot of bunting, and regardless of whether it's a strike or not, you gotta be able to handle the pitch. Commit yourself, get the bat out over the plate, basically catch the baseball with the bat. Get it going in the direction of the first baseman."

Rodriguez crept in from third, but Clark, needing to hold Mueller at first, was back.

"A-Rod almost down his [Bellhorn's] throat...A-Rod ended up about thirty feet from the plate," Castiglione said as Quantrill threw over to first. "Four-four the score. Nobody out, the winning run at first."

Quantrill finally delivered, and Bellhorn did try to bunt, fouling it off.

"That's terrible," Sutcliffe said, disgusted, pointing out Bellhorn's poor bunting technique. "He's very fortunate that he did not make an out."

Rodriguez charged and stood no more than 45 feet from home plate, but Quantrill instead threw to first, Mueller diving back safely. McCarver on FOX offered this observation: "Sometimes when a third baseman does that...it intimidates the hitter and makes the hitter, particularly a left-hander, pay more attention to how shallow you are than bunting the ball. It's a very intimidating play by Rodriguez."

On the next pitch, Bellhorn once again fouled off the bunt attempt, making it 0–2.

"You've got to take the bunt off. He's got no chance of getting it down," Sutcliffe said with an almost sadness in his voice at the lack of fundamentals being displayed. "Watch him stab at it, watch him push at it. You get the bat out there over the plate, over the outer half of the plate, and as the baseball comes into the strike zone, you just 'catch' the baseball with the bat. Now you gotta let him swing, now you gotta hope if you're Francona that he doesn't hit it on the ground at somebody."

There's a saying in sports: sometimes the best trades you make are the ones you don't make. Sometimes the best bunt attempt is the one that leads you to swing away. Down 0–2, Bellhorn now had to swing away, but he gave away two strikes in the process. Rodriguez retreated to his normal double-play depth at third, and Quantrill came to the plate. Bellhorn turned on it and ripped it into right field on a line for a single, moving Mueller to second. Instead of a runner at second with one out, Boston now had runners at first and second with nobody out, and Johnny Damon coming up.

"How to turn a bunt for a sacrifice into a base hit," said McCarver. "On an 0–2 pitch."

"Mark Bellhorn could not get a bunt down to save his life, but on two strikes he tears into a base hit," remarked O'Brien.

Damon, considered the best bat-handler on the Red Sox, looked to the third base coach for a sign. The Yankees had faced a similar situation in the eighth when Cairo led off with a double and Jeter, New York's best bunter and leadoff hitter, sacrificed him to third, setting the table for their 2 and 3 hitters to drive him in.

The bunt was successful, but Rodriguez and Sheffield failed to deliver Cairo. The issue for Francona was that Damon was a .389 hitter off Quantrill, and Cabrera even better at .615.

Everyone got the answer immediately, as Damon squared while Quantrill was still in his set. Clark charged from first base, and Damon popped it up on the infield, where Posada made the catch in front of home plate.

"Boy, the Red Sox in a clinic on how not to bunt at the big-league level," O'Brien said.

"They have to be better at that," said Sutcliffe. "This time of year in particular. You see Derek Jeter get the job done. You've seen other people get down bunts when they have to."

"Damon's had a very, very, very tough series," lamented Trupiano.

Meanwhile, Quantrill was shaken up, and Torre and a trainer paid him a visit. Concerned for his pitcher, who was dealing with a bad right knee, Torre removed him and brought in Esteban Loaiza. The thirty-two-year-old Mexican native was pitching out of the Yankee bullpen for the second straight night, having pitched two shutout innings in Game 4. He had a subpar season in 2004, starting the year with the White Sox before they dealt him to the Yankees. All told, he pitched 183 innings and posted a poor 5.70 ERA with a sky-high 1.57 WHIP. However, the year before, he finished second in the AL Cy Young balloting, going 21–9 with a 2.90 ERA and a league-leading 209 strikeouts over 226.1 quality innings pitched. He clearly had ability and had become a valuable member of the Yankee staff. He had as long as he needed to warm up, as Quantrill had been removed for an injury.

He entered the game in a very tight spot. Runners on first and second, one out, and the Sox' 2 hitter, Orlando Cabrera, up and Manny Ramirez waiting on deck. Finally warm, he got ready to throw. Cabrera dug in, needing just a hit to the outfield to win the game. The crowd, quieted by the long injury delay, came to life again.

Loaiza missed low for ball one. In an ideal world for Loaiza, he'd induce a double-play grounder so he wouldn't have to face Ramirez with the winning run in scoring position. His second pitch was a good fastball low and away that Cabrera poked foul. He missed high with a slider to bring the count to 2–1, and Cabrera was in the driver's seat. On the fourth pitch of the at-bat, Cabrera hit a hard one-hopper to Jeter at short, who fielded it cleanly and slung it to Cairo, who then made a beautiful turn at second and a strong throw to Clark at first to complete the inning-ending double play. Clark actually dug the ball out of the dirt, a play that, had he not made, could have cost New York the game.

Boston, who had two runners on with nobody out, lost out on an absolutely golden opportunity to win the game, and now it would be up to Tim Wakefield, coming out of the Red Sox bullpen, to keep them in the game as they headed for the twelfth.

12

THE TWELFTH INNING

In 1988, the Pittsburgh Pirates drafted a second baseman from Florida Tech with a little power. Tim Wakefield had hit 22 home runs—the single-season record at the small school in Melbourne, Florida. He played for Watertown of the New York–Penn League (NYPL) and batted a paltry .189 with three home runs in 159 at-bats. He was a good athlete, but nothing remarkable. He also struck out 57 times in those 159 at-bats and showed very little promise as a future infielder. A scout told him that he didn't possess the skills necessary to move past the AA level, and, in his first year as a pro ballplayer, he faced a crossroads.

The odds of any player making the major leagues are long. More than three million kids play Little League baseball each year. By the time they reach high school, those three million kids are down to just 483,000 still playing. The winnowing of the field continues as they move to college—just 36,000 play college baseball. Each year, less than 1,200 of those players get drafted. Of that group, just 900 will sign professional contracts. Less than one in five players drafted make the major leagues.

For Wakefield, the odds were even longer, because his first chance to impress fell flat. The Pirates' organization was short on quality pitching, and Wakefield decided that, instead of quitting, he would try one more thing to pursue a baseball career. He didn't have a big-league arm, and so, with few options, he decided to try the knuckleball. "I just wanted to say I tried everything I could to make it," he would later say.

In 1989, his pitching career began, and it was a relative success. He pitched 39.2 innings for the Welland Pirates of the New York–Penn League, posting a 3.40 ERA, and flummoxing minor league hitters by striking out 9.5 per nine innings. He became a starter the next year for Salem, Virginia (A+ level), winning 10 games over 190.1 innings, and then 15 games between AA Carolina and AAA Buffalo in 1991. There was something there. In 1992, he started the year in Buffalo and went 10–3 with a 3.06 ERA and got the call-up to the majors. Incredibly, he posted an 8–1 record with the Pirates, along with a 2.15 ERA, becoming a key contributor to a division-winning Pittsburgh team and receiving the *Sporting News* Rookie of the Year Award. In the NLCS that year, he won both his starts against future Hall of Famer Tom Glavine, including a five-hit complete game victory.

The following year, as he was expected to perform at a high level, it fell apart. He walked 75 batters in just 128.1 innings, posted a 5.61 ERA, and was sent back down to the minors. His struggles continued there in AA Carolina, and then again the following year in AAA Buffalo, where, in 1994, he went 5–15 with a 5.84 ERA. The Pirates cut him loose, and his career appeared to be over.

But Boston picked him up and immediately brought in Phil and Joe Niekro, the famous knuckleballing brothers, and they began to work with Wakefield. In 1995, Boston was in a terrific pennant race and needed help in the rotation. They called him up from AAA Pawtucket, and he responded with another spectacular "rookie" year, going 16–8 (14–1 in the first half, yet he did not make the all-star game) with a 2.95 ERA, good for a third place finish in the AL Cy Young Award balloting. His performance helped Boston win the division.

The next three seasons, his ERA wasn't the same (4.66), but he won 43 games and pitched more than 200 innings each year, providing dependability that Boston needed. Three relatively down years followed until he once again found knuckleball magic in 2002, going 11–5 with a 2.81 ERA. Despite being a starter, in 1999, he did help Boston out of the bullpen, moving into the closer role and recording 15 saves and recording a 3.50 ERA in relief. Incredibly, by the time he finished his career in Boston, he would finish third in franchise history in wins, second in strike-outs, second in appearances, first in games started, and first in innings pitched. Not too bad for a guy who was inches away from being out of baseball after just one season in the minors.

Wakefield made a living throwing an old-time pitch, the knuckleball. It's a pitch that's really misnamed, as it gives the impression that it's thrown with the knuckles pressed against the ball. Tim McCarver, a two-time all-star behind the plate, described in his book, *Tim McCarver's Baseball for Brain Surgeons and Other Fans*, how the pitch was really thrown:

"The knuckleball, a slow technique pitch, isn't thrown with the knuckles but with the fingertips. But calling it a 'fingertip ball' wouldn't be too cool. At least, 'knuckle' describes the movement of the ball. It has no spin if thrown correctly. No one knows how it will move, so it's hard to hit and very hard to catch unless you're a practicing lepidopterist. A knuckleball is one pitch, but it could be fifteen pitches wrapped into one because its movement is unforeseeable.

"When you throw a knuckleball, you're pulling down, as you do with a curveball. Think again of pulling down a window shade.... The worst thing that a knuckleball can do is roll or topple—batters won't miss it because it's so slow. In order to keep it from toppling, the pitcher should use the seam and push the ball rather than throw it. Sometimes the ring finger is involved. Barney Schultz threw the best knuckleball I ever caught, and when a batter saw there was no spin on it, he knew he was in trouble. As Charlie Lau said, 'There are two theories on hitting the knuckler. Unfortunately, neither of them works.'"

Multiple-time all-star John Kruk once said of hitting the dastardly pitch, "I'd rather have my leg cut off than do that all day. You just hope it hits your bat in a good spot." Hall of Famer Ernie Banks spoke about the challenges he had hitting Phil Niekro's fluttering knuckleball, saying, "He simply destroys your timing with that knuckleball. It comes flying in there dipping and hopping like crazy and you just can't hit it."

It was not an easy pitch to throw. Baseball writer Tim Kurkjian once said, "I once asked Charlie Hough, another great knuckleball pitcher, why more pitchers didn't throw a knuckleball. 'Why don't more pitchers throw 95 mph?' Hough shot back. 'Because it's really hard to do!'"

Physicist Robert Adair studied the pitch scientifically. Thrown correctly, the pitch darts this way and that, as air currents move the ball around on its journey to home plate. Even though the pitch is one of the slowest in the game, it's still moving between 60 and 70 miles per hour—as fast as an average car on the highway. Due to the limited reaction time that human physiology can muster, a knuckleball that's dancing moves so quickly that Adair concluded it can only be hit through sheer luck. You have to just swing in a spot and hope that's where the ball will be. It's no wonder that watching the best hitters in the game flail away at a soft knuckleball is like watching a man trapped in a phone booth with a golf club and an angry hornet.

The problem with the knuckleball—well, one of the problems; the other will be discussed later—is that if it isn't thrown correctly, it's the ultimate meatball for a hitter. It might just roll instead of flutter, making it easier to hit than a batting practice pitch. So it's dangerous for pitchers to throw against big-league hitters unless they've got a good feel for it. Alas, if it's moving too much, it can make a knuckleballer become quite wild, resulting in walks.

A knuckleballer coming into the game in relief is an extremely uncertain and dangerous proposition. Francona was well aware of this when he called on Wakefield in the twelfth inning of Game 5, but one advantage he had was that Wakefield could pitch for a long time. He had thrown 64 pitches in relief in Game 3 just two days earlier, offering to eat the innings to aid a beleaguered pitching staff, and once again his rubber arm was called on to do the job. Unfortunately for Wakefield, his recent postseason history against New York wasn't very good.

In 2003, he pitched two terrific games against the Yankees in the ALCS, beating them 5–2 in Game 1, throwing six innings of two-run ball, and then again in Game 4, going seven innings, allowing just one run in a 3–2 victory. But then the roof caved in. In Game 7, he allowed the famous eleventh-inning walk-off and series-losing homer to Aaron Boone. Then in 2004, he gave up three hits and two runs in one inning in the Game 1 loss, then got tattooed for five hits, two walks, and five runs over 3.1 innings in the Game 3 blowout loss. Over his last 5.1 postseason innings against the Yankees, he allowed nine hits, two walks, and eight runs. Now, he was again on the mound with the season on the line.

Tony Clark, fresh off a near game-winning hit in the ninth, led off and swung at a knuckleball that fell off a table, missing it by six inches, for strike one. Clark had plenty of power to drive even slow pitches well out of the ballpark. The next pitch, coming in at 70 miles an hour, was fouled off to the left and out of play, and Wakefield quickly got ahead 0–2. On the third pitch, Clark again waved and missed badly, striking out on three quick pitches.

Miguel Cairo was next up and, on the first pitch he saw, hit a bullet into left field. Ramirez charged but misplayed it, and the ball rolled past him. Cairo, hustling all the way, dug into second and made it easily. It was scored a single plus a one-base error on Ramirez, who was not known for wielding a high-quality glove.

"He was very unsure on that line drive by Cairo," O'Brien noted.

"I honestly thought he should have caught it," Sutcliffe replied. "I thought if he gets a good jump, which Manny doesn't always do, he could have come on in and caught this baseball. He started to come in, then he hesitates, a little too late, and now the Yankees with a runner in scoring position."

The Yankees had the go-ahead run on second with Derek Jeter up. Not the situation Wakefield was looking for, given Jeter's penchant for clutch hits. Wakefield's first pitch dove to the ground, and Jeter let it go for a ball. Varitek had problems securing it, and it rolled past him, but not far enough to allow Cairo to get to third. But the pitch highlighted a challenge facing the Red Sox—could Varitek handle the knuckleball?

Jeter lined the next pitch to right. Kapler got a great jump and raced in to spear the sinking liner to retire Jeter and keep Cairo at second.

"How much more can the nervous system take?" Castiglione asked.

"I'll tell you what, my gray hairs are getting gray hairs," Trupiano replied.

Rodriguez was next. On the first pitch, he hit a hard liner to fairly deep center, but Damon had it lined up all the way, retreated, and made a somewhat difficult catch look routine. Wakefield quickly worked around the one-out hit and error, and Boston came up with yet another chance to win the game.

MANNY RAMIREZ LED off the bottom of the twelfth for Boston. Ramirez would retire as one of the greatest right-handed hitters of all time, and a brief look at his career stats tells you why: .312 average, .996 OPS, 555 home runs, 1,831 RBIs, 1,544 runs, 154 OPS+. He led the league in homers, RBIs, batting average, on-base percentage (three times), slugging (three times), OPS (three times), and OPS+. He twice led in intentional walks received. Though he never won an MVP, he finished in the top 12 of MVP voting 10 times, including eight years in a row, and finished top 5 four times. He won eight Silver Slugger Awards.

In his four-year peak from 1999 to 2002, he hit .333, with a .437 OBP, 1.089 OPS, 176 OPS+, 156 homers, and 519 RBIs. Just a ridiculous offensive résumé.

He was also a terrific postseason performer. In 111 games, he hit .285 with a .937 OPS, 29 homers, and 78 RBIs. Project those numbers out over 150 games and you're looking at 39 home runs and 105 RBIs—against the best pitching a hitter will face all season long.

Later in 2007 and 2008, he would have two amazing post-season runs. The first was with Boston, as they went on to win the World Series. In 14 postseason games that year, he hit .348 with a 1.160 OPS, with four homers and 16 RBIs. And in eight games for the Dodgers the next year, he hit .520 with a 1.747 OPS, with four homers and 10 RBIs. He was a true savant with the bat, and for his entire career, he was one of the most feared hitters in the game.

He retired after the 2011 season. The waiting period for Hall of Fame entry is five years, so the question is: Why isn't a player like Manny Ramirez in the Hall of Fame? The answer is simple: steroids. Like Alex Rodriguez, Ramirez was twice caught using performance-enhancing drugs, and for some sportswriters (the gatekeepers to Cooperstown), that has always been a reason to keep obviously HOF-level players like Ramirez, Rodriguez, Clemens, and Bonds out of the Hall.

In 2009, MLB informed Ramirez that he would be suspended 50 games for violating their drug policy. He claimed that a physician had prescribed a banned medication by accident, but he decided not to challenge the suspension. He was found to have used human chorionic gonadotropin (hCG), a woman's fertility drug that steroid users often employed to restart their normal testosterone production after coming off a steroid cycle. Jason

Giambi and other clients of BALCO had used similar products. Moreover, Ramirez was found to have artificial testosterone in his body as well.

In 2011, MLB again informed Ramirez that he faced a suspension. This time, it would be 100 games for a second offense. His first drug test came back positive, and he appealed, but his second test also came back positive. He dropped the appeal and promptly retired. He would later try to come back, but he never saw the majors again.

Ben Buchanan wrote in 2016 for "Over the Monster," comparing Ramirez to Bonds and Clemens, "But even if those two do manage to make their way to Cooperstown, that's no guarantee for Ramirez. While it's true that Clemens and Bonds making the hall would guarantee there's enough voters willing to consider steroid users to carry a candidate, and Ramirez' accomplishments should clearly be enough for all of those voters to consider him worthy of the hall if they're willing to overlook his PED use, the reality is that his transgressions are not the same as those of Bonds and Clemens. Ramirez was not simply a product of the steroid era, going along with what everyone else was doing. While his late violations at least allow the possibility that much of his career was legitimate, they also remove any chance to write off his transgressions as part of a shameful period in league history that could maybe be blamed on the game as a whole rather than just the individuals. It's like breaking the speed limit. Sure, you're not technically supposed to go 65 in a 55, but there's more people on I-95 breaking the limit than obeying it. Take that 65 and put it on the streets of Arlington, on the other hand, and suddenly we have a very real problem."

Players like Ramirez, Rodriguez, Clemens, and Bonds were great players—steroids or not. But their legacies are certainly tainted, and none of them have been voted into the Hall of Fame. Could they someday? It's possible, depending on how voters feel with more time and distance from these players' careers. But there is no denying their talent, and at the moment, Manny Ramirez stood in the batter's box staring out at Esteban Loaiza.

On the 1–0 count, Ramirez took a massive cut at a low fastball and fouled it back. It was the kind of pitch that Manny often sent flying, but he just missed it. On the next pitch, Loaiza threw a 90 mph fastball above the belt over the heart of the plate, and Ramirez sent a sky-high pop-up on the shallow infield. Rodriguez came in, the ball swirling in the air, and made a fairly difficult catch to retire Ramirez.

"Rodriguez for just a moment took his eye off it to make sure Posada wasn't bearing down on him, and there's one down with Ortiz coming up," Buck said.

"You know in the eighth inning, you remarked about how identical this game seemed to last night's game," McCarver said. "And here we are in the twelfth inning, and who's the batter but David Ortiz, who won it for the Sox last night."

Loaiza's first pitch to Big Papi was a fastball drilling the outside corner for a strike. He missed farther outside to even the count and then pumped a 93 mph fastball on the outside corner for a strike. He was staying away from Ortiz, not wanting to come inside so Ortiz could pull the ball. On the 1–2 pitch, Loaiza barely missed with a slider low that somehow Ortiz didn't swing at. An underrated aspect of Ortiz' game had always been his ability to work the count and take tough pitches just off the plate. He led the league in walks in 2006 and 2007, demonstrating a superb eye.

Fans nervously clapped, hoping Ortiz would send one flying over the Monster in left. Loaiza finally came inside with a fastball but missed high and tight, and the count was full. Ortiz drew a walk as Loaiza missed down and away, another pitch that was very close.

The question Francona now faced was whether to pinch-run for Ortiz. One of the team's slowest runners, he was perhaps the least likely player to steal a base or advance an extra base on a hit. Boston still had Pokey Reese and Doug Mirabelli on the bench. Mirabelli would not be used, as he was as slow as Ortiz, a far worse hitter, and the only backup catcher on the roster. Reese, however, was a fast middle infielder (he stole a career-high 38 bases in 1999) and would be a terrific choice to put in to run for Ortiz. But with one out, was it worth taking Ortiz' bat out of the lineup should the game be extended? Francona weighed the options and stuck with Ortiz.

Meanwhile, Torre had a decision of his own to make—whether to keep Loaiza in the game. Sutcliffe pointed this out, saying, "Not many options left for either manager. Javier Vázquez, the only guy listed as possibly available in the bullpen for Joe Torre tonight. What that means is that Esteban Loaiza, I don't know if you're gonna win it, I don't know if you're gonna lose it, but son, you're gonna complete it, one way or the other."

Doug Mientkiewicz stepped into the box, hoping to duplicate his last at-bat, when he sent a rocket over the head of Gary Sheffield in right for a double. Loaiza fired a series of fastballs and cut fastballs, and the count became 2–1. At this point, Francona decided to play one of his cards. Not wanting Mientkiewicz to hit into a double play, and figuring he'd get a good pitch to hit on a 2–1 count, he surprisingly signaled a steal for Ortiz, who only had about a three-foot lead off first.

The pitch was a strike, on the outside corner at the knees—a tough pitch to hit for Mientkiewicz. Posada came up firing and launched a throw that Jeter had to leap to catch. Ortiz half slid, half stumbled into second base as Jeter came down, swiping at Ortiz with his glove. Second-base umpire Randy Marsh called Ortiz out, and the crowd—shocked at first to see Ortiz running—erupted. It looked like Ortiz had managed to get under the tag, forced high by Posada's errant throw.

Ortiz began screaming at Marsh. Francona sprinted—if it could be called that—out of the dugout to argue.

"I'm not sure he tagged him," McCarver said during the replay. "I think the hand was in there. I don't think Jeter tagged him."

"You get a good look at it here," Buck replied as another angle appeared on the FOX broadcast.

"I think the hand was on the bag, by the time Jeter's glove came down on his back," McCarver said.

"I agree," said Buck. "Looked like he got him by the end, down on the lower back, and Ortiz' hand was on the base."

On MLB, Sutcliffe said, "Terry Francona may have an argument here. Papi looked like he got underneath the tag....one of the ugliest slides you're ever gonna see."

"Where was Ortiz going?" asked Trupiano. "Did somebody miss a hit-and-run sign?"

"Had to be a missed sign," Castiglione replied.

Every replay appeared to show Ortiz sliding safely, except one—a view from center field that looked as if Jeter was able to apply the tag just before Ortiz' hand hit the bag. Either way, it was an incredibly close play that went in New York's favor. One pitch later, Mientkiewicz struck out to end the inning.

The two teams headed to the thirteenth inning, still tied at four.

13

THE THIRTEENTH INNING

Bob Uecker famously once said, "The way to catch a knuckleball is to wait until it stops rolling and then pick it up." Tim McCarver, in his book *Tim McCarver's Baseball for Brain Surgeons and Other Fans*, told the story of an all-star-caliber catcher struggling mightily to handle a knuckleball. He wrote,

> "In the 1986 All-Star game, Charlie Hough was pitching in the eighth inning with the winning run on third. Rich Gedman was the catcher, and though he hadn't experienced catching a knuckler with regularity, he felt obliged to call for Hough's dominant pitch. It took courage. I saw that Gedman was opening his

right hand next to the glove on each pitch. It was actually farther ahead than his glove. That's what often happens—you want to stab at the ball before it bites you. That is a sign that the catcher's arms aren't relaxed, and it's hard to have the gloved left hand relaxed when the right hand is stiff. Understandably, Gedman didn't realize that the arms have to be back close to the body and loose to catch a knuckler, so he was just inviting a wild pitch. The viewers were alerted and, not surprisingly, two pitches later the run scored on a wild pitch and the National League won, 4–3."

To be sure, a knuckleball can be hard to hit, but often it can be hard to catch as well. In an interview for FOX sports, catcher Russell Martin spoke of his attempts to catch R. A. Dickey's tough knuckler: "I feel like it's going to be tough every time. R. A.'s knuckleball, it's tough to follow. You never know what it's going to do. But the more you catch him, the more repetitions you get, the better it is. The more you work at it, the easier it gets. Sal [Butera] actually helped me, in the setup and how to position myself to feel more comfortable behind the plate. The one thing he told me was to just relax. And don't try to follow the ball with the glove the whole way. Wait for the ball to get to a certain area, then commit. Keeping the arm relaxed helps a lot. My first bullpen I caught R. A., my shoulder was burning after like 30 pitches. I was like, 'What's going on?' I guess I'm not used to doing that with the glove. So, keep it relaxed. Make your move at the last second."

No less an authority than Joe Torre once said, "You don't catch the knuckleball, you defend against it." He knew as well as anyone how difficult it was to catch someone like Tim Wakefield.

For Boston, the duty of catching Wakefield in the thirteenth inning fell to starter Jason Varitek. Varitek, like his Yankee counterpart Jorge Posada, played nonstop during the ALCS, including back-to-back-to-back brutally long games. Not only long, but the last two were incredibly high stress. And Varitek was not Boston's normal battery mate for Wakefield. That job usually went to Doug Mirabelli, who had become somewhat of an expert knuckleball receiver. It was a job so specialized that two years later, after Mirabelli had been gone, the Red Sox discovered that they desperately needed him back to catch Wakefield; and so general manager Theo Epstein traded with San Diego to reacquire Mirabelli. But there was urgency, because that very night, Wakefield was scheduled to pitch.

Mirabelli arrived at Boston's Logan Airport on May 1, 2006, following the trade. His plane landed twelve minutes before game time. His pilot had to clear airspace on the flight path, a very unusual procedure. In order to get him to Fenway on time, Boston police were dispatched to provide an escort. Mirabelli changed into his uniform in the car as they sped down Boston streets to the park. He made it to the park just in time and helped Wakefield pitch seven quality innings in a 7–3 victory over the Yankees.

Mirabelli sat on the bench in Game 5, however, and it was up to Varitek to secure Wakefield's wobbly pitches. Former umpire Ron Luciano said, "Like some cult religion that barely survives, there has always been at least one but rarely more than five or six devotees throwing the knuckleball in the big leagues...Not only can't pitchers control it, hitters can't hit it, catchers can't catch it, coaches can't coach it, and most pitchers can't learn it. The perfect pitch."

Varitek was well aware of the challenge he faced. Just the inning before, he had difficulty catching one of Wakefield's knucklers. He truly would have no idea what was in store for him in the thirteenth inning of Game 5.

Slugger Gary Sheffield led off against Wakefield. Over his career, Sheffield had modest success against the knuckleballer, hitting .235 with two homers and eight walks in 34 at-bats. In the series so far, Sheffield had doubled off Wakefield in Game 1, doubled again in Game 3, and added a single in Game 3. To this point in his career, he was 7–19 against Wakefield. Wakefield simply couldn't get him out during the series.

Wakefield's first two pitches were out of the strike zone, and on the second, Sheffield checked his swing, coming close to a strike. Wakefield finally got one over before throwing a pitch that dropped a foot, and Sheffield missed by even more. A ball in the dirt made the count full. Sheffield dug in for the payoff pitch. He swung and missed badly, but the ball moved so much that Varitek never actually even got a glove on it. It ricocheted off his arm and chest protector and went all the way to the backstop. Sheffield realized that the ball got away and hustled to first base. Varitek chased it down but had no chance of making a play. Wakefield had gotten the strikeout, but Sheffield stood on first on a passed ball.

"You see that a lot with knuckleballers on strikeouts," O'Brien said. "That's how it goes into the scorebook."

Sutcliffe noted, "What you don't see a lot of is Jason Varitek catching Tim Wakefield. That's normally Doug Mirabelli's job."

Matsui was next, and now a passed ball would get Sheffield into scoring position. Varitek had to be sweating bullets behind the plate. Wakefield motioned to Varitek to relax. He didn't need his catcher tense back there.

"Oh, what a tough way for the Red Sox to give up a base. The leadoff man is on," said Castiglione.

"Wouldn't you know it would be something squirrelly like that in a grinding game like this?" Trupiano replied.

Wakefield threw over to first twice in a row, just trying to keep Sheffield close. Sheffield was getting older but still had decent speed. As late as 2003, he stole 18 bases, and against a pitcher like Wakefield, stolen bases were much easier to come by. Not only did the pitch take longer to get to the catcher, there was a much greater chance that the catcher wouldn't receive the ball cleanly, making it more difficult to make a good throw.

A ball and a strike made it 1–1, with Sheffield showing no signs of running. Another throw to first. Ball two was in the dirt, and Varitek did a good job keeping it in front of him. Another ball made it 3–1, and suddenly Wakefield was in trouble. Now might be the time for him to throw a "fastball"—a straight pitch that could reach as high as 80 mph, certainly far too slow to be a major league–level fastball, but if it caught the hitter by surprise, it could work. And if it didn't...

He threw a knuckler instead, and Matsui hit a ground ball to Bellhorn at second. It was slow enough so that Sheffield had a chance to advance unless Bellhorn played it cleanly. He did, and managed to get the force at second, and now the Yankees had a slower runner at first and one out.

Bernie Williams next stepped into the box and took the first pitch for a strike, and then one down and in for a ball to make the count 1–1. Another Wakefield knuckler, and Williams sent one to relatively deep right center, but Kapler drifted over and made a routine play. Matsui jogged back to first and Kapler fired the ball to Mientkiewicz, forcing Matsui to hustle back to safety. Two outs.

Jorge Posada came up, batting left-handed. Occasionally, switch-hitters would bat right-handed against knuckleball pitchers, but both Williams and Posada chose the left side. The first pitch was a harder knuckleball that looked like a strike, but it glanced off Varitek's glove and bounced away. It wasn't far enough to advance Matsui, but it was far enough to perhaps distract Kellogg and fool him into thinking it was a ball, and the count was 1–0. Wakefield next dropped a slower version in for the first strike of the at-bat.

"And a skittish Jason Varitek behind the plate," said McCarver. "Understandably."

"And…that's why," Buck said as the next pitch—a ball—deflected off Varitek's wrist and rolled to the fence. Varitek ran it down as Matsui advanced to second base on the second passed ball of the inning for the catcher.

"That knuckleball is really dancing tonight," McCarver said. "This went off the heel of the glove. The one to Sheffield never hit leather and hit him on the wrist."

"Well, this is a decision that Francona decided to make," O'Brien said, "not to bring in Mirabelli, to stay with Varitek."

Varitek would say later in his career, "You know, catching the knuckleball, it's like trying to catch a fly with a chopstick."

Russell Martin, in the interview referenced earlier, had said, "Any time there is [sic] two strikes, any time there are men on base, you've got to lock it in completely." At this point, Varitek had already missed four pitches. Two of them didn't roll far enough away for any runner to move up 90 feet, but he knew he was in trouble back there.

Boston decided to walk Posada to put runners at first and second and take their chances with Rubén Sierra. Sierra was 2 for 15 lifetime against Wakefield, "And that's the best reason why Posada just got the free pass," said Buck.

Paul Flannery recalled watching the game and wrote for SB Nation, "Ah, the 13th. Nothing bad can happen here. Sheffield is swinging for the Mass Pike. He's legitimately terrifying. Somehow,

Wakefield strikes out Sheffield with a nasty knuckler that Varitek misplays into a passed ball. I remember thinking at the time, *This is how it's going to happen. This is how they're going to kill us.* Two outs now and Matsui's at first. Whoops, another passed ball. Now he's at second. Intentional walk to Posada. Everyone at Fenway is nervous as hell. My wife comes into the room and starts watching. Now she's nervous."

The first pitch was a strike, and Varitek held on cleanly. The crowd stood, the volume rising. Sierra fouled the next pitch back for strike two, and the noise increased, the fans hoping to will the inning to be over. The next pitch was inside, and Varitek had to reach over and backhand it. Everywhere in New England, hearts nearly stopped. The count was 1–2.

"It can be both terrifying and courageous of a catcher calling for the knuckleball here," said McCarver. "You have to call for it, but then once you call for it, you have to catch it."

Sierra fouled one back to stay alive in the at-bat. Boston fans knew their season hung by a thread here.

"Varitek is just happy right now, Al Leiter, that there isn't anybody standing on third base," Buck said.

Wakefield unleashed a darting, floating knuckleball that drifted outside. Varitek stabbed at it, but it deflected off his glove and rolled all the way to the backstop, which, as Leiter pointed out, was quite a ways behind home plate. Matsui went to third, and Posada went to second. New York was one more passed ball away from taking the lead and likely winning the game.

"Three passed balls," said Castiglione. "Two men in scoring position."

"You still have to call the knuckleball," McCarver said.

"And you think there was pressure on him [Varitek] before," Sutcliffe said on MLB. "He's doing everything he can."

On the 2–2 pitch, Wakefield's knuckler was high for ball three, and even on that one, Varitek couldn't squeeze it. It popped out of his mitt and bounced a short distance away, not nearly far enough for Matsui to score, but enough to make it feel like he would never catch another pitch. Another passed ball at this point seemed like a fait accompli, and it was just a matter of when.

On the 3–2, Wakefield threw a dazzling knuckleball, dancing all over. Sierra swung and missed. Varitek held on like it was playing catch with a Little Leaguer. Easy as pie, as if all the other crazy deflections had never happened. The Fenway crowd erupted, cheering Wakefield and maybe even more so, Varitek.

Chad Finn wrote for the *Boston Globe*, "Now, perhaps the unfamiliar and uninformed might look at the box score from this game, notice that Varitek had three passed balls in a single inning, and wonder how we could praise his performance so definitively. But you know why, don't you? He was catching knuckleballer Wakefield—a very rare assignment for him even though they were teammates for 15 seasons—and Wake had the knuckleball *dancing* like a disco queen on this night. I'm not sure there has been a tenser half inning in Red Sox history than the top of the 13th in this game."

Bill Simmons in his book, *Now I Can Die in Peace*, wrote of that harrowing experience as a fan, "In either the 13th or 14th— God I can't even remember, it's all a blur—Wakefield struck out Sheffield on a passed ball, followed by another walk and another passed ball. Suddenly they had runners on second and third with two outs, with only a 50 percent chance that Varitek could stop these knuckleballs. Apparently, we got out of this mess. I'm pretty sure I blacked out. I'm not even kidding.

"My last three notes of the game: '13th inning oh my God Varitek and Wakefield'...'Stand up sit down bad back'...'Central nervous system shutting down.' If they found me dead outside Fenway after the game, they would have examined this thing and assumed I had died of natural causes."

It's hard to describe the tension in Fenway Park at the time. Viewing it now doesn't come close to capturing it, because rewatching it, baseball fans know how the game is going to turn out.

Somehow they escaped without losing the lead.

THE BOTTOM OF the thirteenth was far less eventful. Loaiza, suddenly looking sharp, mowed down Kapler, Varitek, and Mueller with the help of some terrific defense. Kapler hit a bullet back up the middle, but Loaiza snared it for the first out. Varitek, who had been kept in the game because he was a much better hitter than Mirabelli, hit a weak routine grounder to short, and Jeter threw him out easily. With two out, Mueller skied an 0–2 pitch into shallow left. Jeter sprinted out, Matsui sprinted in, and a split second before they collided, Matsui reached out to pick it from the air, making the final out and avoiding catastrophe. Loaiza retired the side in order on just nine pitches. Just like that, the Yankees were coming up again, and Wakefield headed to the mound, with Varitek suited up behind the plate, chopsticks at the ready.

14

THE FOURTEENTH INNING

Games 4 and 5 represented the fourth time the Red Sox had ever been in two extra-inning playoff games in the same series. In 1986, Boston lost Game 4 to the Angels, 4–3, in 11 innings, completing a stirring comeback from three runs down in the bottom of the ninth inning. Roger Clemens had been pitching brilliantly for eight shutout innings and then gave up a home run and two singles. Manager John McNamara brought in closer Calvin Schiraldi, who promptly gave up a double that allowed two runs and tied the game. Schiraldi finished the ninth, then pitched the tenth, and came out for the eleventh, in which he gave up the winning run on a Bobby Grich single.

The next day, in Game 5, Boston turned the tables. Down three games to one and facing elimination, Boston trailed 5–1 going into the top of the ninth inning. The Red Sox rallied, getting a single by Bill Buckner and a home run from ex-Angel Don Baylor to cut the lead to two, and then a hit-by-pitch of Sox' catcher Rich Gedman set the stage for one of Boston's all-time biggest moments. Dave Henderson launched a Donnie Moore pitch over the fence for a game-tying two-run homer. They would go on to win it in the eleventh on a Henderson sacrifice fly. Boston would win the series in seven games, and for Moore, the ninth inning in Game 5 would change his life in a tragic way. On July 18, 1989, he took his own life in an apparent suicide.

"Ever since he gave up the home run to Dave Henderson he was never himself again," said Dave Pinter, Moore's longtime agent, following his death. "He blamed himself for the Angels not going to the World Series. He constantly talked about the Henderson home run. It was that important to him that the Angels make it to the World Series. He couldn't get over it. I tried to get him to go to a psychiatrist, but he said, 'I don't need it, I'll get over it.' Even when he was told that one pitch doesn't make a season, he couldn't get over it. That home run killed him."

Former teammate Brian Downing placed the blame on a sports media that hounded Moore following the loss: "Everything revolved around one...pitch. You [the media] destroyed a man's life over one pitch. The guy was just not the same after that. You buried the guy. He was never treated fairly. He wasn't given credit for all the good things he did. Nobody was sympathetic. It was always, 'He's jaking it, he's fooling around.' He was a very sensitive guy. I never, ever saw the guy credited for getting us to the play-offs, because all you ever heard about, all you ever read about was one...pitch."

Boston would go on to lose the World Series, in part due to one of their own collapses, a Game 6 loss to the Mets that forever haunted another player—Red Sox' first baseman Bill Buckner—but without the same tragic result.

In 1975, Boston played two extra-inning games against the Cincinnati Reds in the World Series. Boston lost Game 3, 6–5, in 10 innings, after staging a remarkable comeback to tie the game in the ninth. And Game 6, a 7–6 Boston victory, has gone down as one of the greatest baseball games in World Series history, and in fact, in all of baseball history. It is immortalized by Carlton Fisk's dramatic twelfth-inning home run off the left field foul pole, and by the camera shot of him waving his arms, willing the ball to stay fair.

The famous shot was part accident, part planning by NBC. They had developed a new camera placement for games in Fenway, inside the manual scoreboard within the Green Monster itself. They wanted the angle to be more in left center, but support beams and the human scoreboard operator (Fenway has one of the last remaining manually operated scoreboards in MLB) were in the way, so they were forced to place the camera more toward the left field foul line. Louis Gerard was the cameraman who got the famous shot. He once explained how it happened. Gerard said that director Harry Coyle told him to follow the ball if Fisk hit it.

Gerard replied, "'Harry, I can't. I've got a rat on my leg that's as big as a cat. It's staring me in the face. I'm blocked by a piece of metal on my right.' So he said, 'What are we going to do?' I said, 'How about if we stay with Fisk, see what happens?'"

And so one of baseball's most iconic moments was captured thanks to some thoughtfulness on the NBC crew, the construction of the Green Monster, and some rats.

In 2003, another year in which Boston played two extra-inning playoff games in the same series, Boston lost Game 1 of the

ALDS to Oakland, 5–4, in 12 innings, as the A's tied the game in the ninth when Erubiel Durazo singled off Alan Embree, and then won it in the twelfth on a successful squeeze bunt by Ramón Hernández. Down two games to none, Boston stayed alive in Game 3 by winning 3–1 in 11 innings, thanks to a two-run walk-off homer by Trot Nixon.

The 2004 series against the Yankees featured back-to-back dramatic extra-inning games. In Game 4, Boston came back against Mariano Rivera, with the Millar walk, the Roberts steal, the Mueller single, and then in the twelfth inning, the Ortiz walk-off home run. And on this night, less than twenty-four hours later, the teams were locked in a duel for the ages, New York desperately trying to close out the series, and Boston frantically trying to stay alive. Both managers had used up nearly all of their bullets in the bullpen. Joe Torre had gone through seven pitchers and was expecting Loaiza to go as long as possible. The Game 2 starter, Jon Lieber, was already on his way to New York to rest and prepare for a Game 6 start, if needed. If New York had won and clinched the pennant, he would have missed the celebration. Boston had also used seven pitchers, and Wakefield was in the same position as Loaiza. Unlike Lieber, Boston's presumptive Game 6 starter, Curt Schilling, was in the bullpen, ready to be used if necessary. Francona hoped it wouldn't be necessary, for then he had no Game 6 starter yet identified. But that would be a problem he'd have to deal with later. For now, winning Game 5 was the priority. Just in case, Francona had the last member of his bullpen, Curtis Leskanic, warming.

Wakefield, coming off a harrowing thirteenth inning, prepared to face Clark, Cairo, and then the top of New York's order. It was imperative to get the 8 and 9 batters. If they got on base with Jeter and A-Rod coming up, it spelled huge trouble for Wakefield.

Varitek, for his part, steeled himself for another inning catching Wakefield's dancing knuckleball.

Clark swung and missed on a knuckler for strike one, and on the very next pitch, he swung and missed again, and Varitek nearly whiffed catching the ball. It barely touched the end of his glove and rolled all the way to the backstop. That couldn't have eased Varitek's nerves.

Buck said, "Wakefield to this point has been almost unhittable." McCarver replied, "Unhittable and uncatchable."

The third pitch didn't move much, and Clark launched one deep into the night. It flew down the right field line, easy home run distance, but curved foul, bouncing off the upper-deck facade. It was another heart-stopping moment, but in the end, it was harmless.

"That's about as far as you'll see a ball hit in this ballpark and not leave the yard," Trupiano said on the radio broadcast.

On another 0–2 pitch, Wakefield lofted a fluttering knuckler that hit the outside corner for strike three. Clark disagreed with the call, as it appeared to be high, but at 6'8", his strike zone was bigger than most, and he headed for the dugout.

Cairo was next and on a 1–0 pitch, Wakefield threw a perfect strike, but the ball was moving so much that even with no swing, Varitek couldn't handle the pitch. Once again, it deflected off his glove and rolled to the backstop. It genuinely looked like a Little League catcher trying to receive pitches. Nearly every other pitch was getting by Varitek, an otherwise excellent defensive catcher. On the 1–1, Cairo crushed one to left, but it, too, was foul. Just a loud strike. Wakefield's next delivery was golfed off the shoe tops into center, a routine catch for Damon. Two out.

That brought up Jeter. Wakefield did not want to face Rodriguez with a runner on base. He did not want Varitek to have to receive his knuckler with Jeter, a fast and excellent base runner, on first.

"We've been at this so long," Buck deadpanned, "that our blimp had to go home."

Jeter swung and missed at the first pitch for strike one. The next swing produced a routine grounder to shortstop, and Cabrera gobbled it up and made a strong throw to first to retire Jeter. Wakefield had gotten through three innings without giving up a run. Despite some nerve-racking moments, he and Varitek had come through huge.

It was now up to Boston's bats in the bottom of the fourteenth.

MARK BELLHORN HAD swung a good bat all game long, but his best would be ahead of him still. On this at-bat, however, he was back to his old ways in the series. Interestingly, the line score read:

NY—4 runs, 12 hits, 1 error
Bos—4 runs, 12 hits, 1 error

It was as even a game as one could imagine. Bellhorn worked the count to 2–2, then Loaiza threw a nasty cut fastball down and in that Bellhorn swung at and missed. Through 2.2 innings, Loaiza had yet to give up a hit, and his cutter, a pitch he discovered the previous year, was biting.

"He's throwing tonight like the guy who pitched last year for the Chicago White Sox," said Sutcliffe. "Look at that late movement down and in."

Damon, anxious to generate any kind of offense, was next. Loaiza started him off with a fastball away for ball one. Another fastball away just missed off the plate to make the count 2–0. After a strike, Loaiza missed again outside to make it 3–1. And on the next pitch, he missed in the same location for ball four. Each ball was in virtually the same spot off the outside corner, and Damon, who O'Brien and Sutcliffe suggested be replaced by Dave Roberts, drew a walk.

Boston had a speedy runner on base with Cabrera coming up. The last time Boston had Damon on first was in the ninth inning, and he got cut down stealing on a great throw by Posada. Would Francona send him again? With one out, a sacrifice was not in play. Maybe a hit-and-run?

"Cabrera, the most apt player in the lineup to use the hit-and-run with," McCarver said. "If the count gets in his favor. One and oh, two and one."

Red Sox fans stood, but the noise was not overwhelmingly loud. It was more of a nervous background hum. Some chanting. Fingers were crossed.

Cabrera swung and missed on the first pitch and then fouled Loaiza's next pitch off Posada's face mask. That took away the hit-and-run and put Cabrera in an 0–2 hole. Now New York could pitch out, which meant that Damon would be less likely to run.

"Cabrera has a tendency to overswing," Trupiano pointed out.

"You don't need a home run here," Castiglione replied.

Loaiza wasted a pitch low and away, hoping to get Cabrera to chase, but no dice. Now at 1–2, Loaiza threw another cutter, and Cabrera swung for the fences and came away empty for strike three. There were two outs. Loaiza and the Yankees were one out away from sending it to the fifteenth inning.

"Everybody's trying to be the hero," Sutcliffe said, "trying to hit it out of the ballpark. That's David Ortiz' gig."

That brought up Manny Ramirez, who did not yet have an RBI in the series. Even with two outs, this was Boston's chance.

Fast runner at first, and Ramirez up with Ortiz on deck, against a pitcher who had thrown a lot of pitches the past couple of nights.

Loaiza started him off with a fastball that missed down and in for ball one. Again, Damon might be on the move, and Loaiza and Posada had to pay attention. But they had to do so without losing focus on one of the game's most dangerous hitters. Loaiza threw to first to keep Damon close. Then a second throw to first, hoping to shorten his lead.

"We talked about at this stage of a ball game," O'Brien said, "closing in on six hours old...how hard you have to try to keep your mental focus. On the mound, in the box, in the field. And the men in the dugout."

Loaiza then came to the plate, and Ramirez fouled a cutter off into the Red Sox' dugout for strike one.

Leiter said, "I wonder with the time he spends with Rivera in the bullpen...he's throwing an awfully good cutter. Many of those pitches that are running away on Cabrera, they were cut fastballs."

Sutcliffe said, "Joe Torre has to like what he's seen. He's had good velocity, good location. He found the same thing out about Javier Vázquez here in this series."

Loaiza then missed inside with a "front-door" cutter that started at Ramirez and came back toward the plate. On 2–1, he threw the exact same pitch, but this time it nipped the inside corner. Ramirez lurched back, thinking it might be too far inside, but it tailed back over the edge of the plate to even the count at 2–2.

"That was a relative of that previous pitch," McCarver said.

Ramirez fouled the next one off to keep the count even.

"Manny! Manny! Manny!" the crowd chanted.

Loaiza had been pounding Ramirez inside and now had him set up for a cutter down and away. Ramirez got it, but it was too far away, and Ramirez let it go for ball three.

"Damon's going to be pushing the envelope," Sutcliffe said, "here with the count full and two outs, he will be off and going with the first movement towards home by Loaiza." The pitch was high for ball four, and suddenly Boston had the winning run at second with Ortiz coming up.

"Now a little old hit would win it," Trupiano said. "Damon to second, he's in scoring position on the walk to Ramirez."

Sutcliffe suggested that perhaps Torre consider intentionally walking Ortiz to pitch to Mientkiewicz. It was not as silly a suggestion as it might seem at first. The advantages and disadvantages to either strategy were obvious. The disadvantages were that it would advance the winning run to third base, where a hit, an error, a walk, or even a wild pitch or a balk would cost New York the game. There were so many more ways to lose a game with a runner at third than with a runner at second. Moreover, Loaiza had struggled with his control over the second half of the season, walking 5.5 batters per nine innings with New York (26 in 42.1 innings as a Yankee), and he had walked three in 3.1 innings in this game. But the advantages were also clear: Ortiz was a far superior hitter to Mientkiewicz in every way.

A third strategy was also possible: pitching around Ortiz. Keep throwing pitches out of the strike zone and hope that an impatient Ortiz would chase. If he did, you'd probably get him out. But if he didn't, you could live with the bases loaded and having to deal with Mientkiewicz. Given that in Ortiz' previous at-bat they stayed away, away, away, it was likely that this is how they'd approach him again, hoping to induce a bad swing or two from the slugging lefty.

"Joe Torre used to talk, when he was in St. Louis," Buck said, "he had Lee Smith as his closer, that once he handed the ball to big Lee he was finished managing. In some respects, it's the same tonight with Loaiza, the last guy the Yankees have in their bullpen. It's Loaiza's game to win or lose."

The first pitch was a good fastball off the outside corner that Ortiz took a massive cut at and missed for strike one.

"Good fastball in a good spot," McCarver said, seeing the ball tail away from Ortiz' bat.

"Ortiz, the hero last night," Trupiano said. "The hero in Game 3 of the league divisional series. Can he be the hero in Game 5? He would settle for a hit to get the winning run home."

The 0–1 pitch missed way outside for ball one.

Buck offered, "You say, be careful with Ortiz, well, you can be, but I told you about the stats this year for Loaiza, all the walks. He's walked three since coming in, two in this inning."

Posada set up outside and Loaiza threw maybe his worst pitch of the night, an 88 mph fastball down the heart of the plate at the knees, missing the target by a good foot or more. Ortiz' eyes lit up and he took a big hack, but only managed to foul it straight back.

"That may have been the most hittable pitch the Red Sox have had from Loaiza in his outing. That ball, the fat part of the plate," McCarver noted.

New York faced a conundrum in the outfield. Ortiz was a power-hitter and was quite likely to hit a fly ball to a deep part of the park. Damon was a speedy runner, already in scoring position. If the Yankees' outfield played back, they could make sure to turn a fly ball into an inning-ending out instead of a game-losing hit. If they played shallow, they could cut off Damon from scoring on a single, but a fly ball that otherwise could be caught might fall in for a game-losing hit. Torre elected to keep them deep.

On the 1–2, Loaiza again went to the outside corner with a fastball. Ortiz managed to get a piece of it and slap it foul down the third base line, staying alive.

Loaiza then tried a typical pitch that often gets left-handed hitters out, a hard slider down and in on the hands. Ortiz dropped the head of the bat and crushed the ball, very high, very far, and deep into the Boston night.

Foul.

The Fenway faithful groaned. Was that their chance?

"The crowd got excited," Sutcliffe said, "but all you had to do was watch David. He never left the batter's box. The baseball left and went a long ways, but he knew right off the bat it had no chance of staying fair."

Not wanting to come inside again, Loaiza went back to the fastball away, missing for ball two. Francona paced in the dugout. Torre sat, looking on stoically. He was ending this game with Loaiza, one way or the other.

"This is now the longest game in postseason history at five hours, forty-seven minutes," Castiglione said.

"If I had confetti, I'd throw it," Trupiano replied sarcastically.

Loaiza once again missed, this pitch a fastball up in the zone. Ortiz tried to crush it, but again only managing to foul it back. That prompted a visit to the mound from Posada.

The next pitch was better, at the belt and away, but this time Ortiz did a good job spoiling the pitch, fouling it off to the left. Loaiza, above the 30-pitch mark in the inning—well over the 15-pitch league average per inning—was trying to figure out how to get Ortiz out. Ortiz, meanwhile, was trying to figure out how to solve Loaiza. 35,120 fans chanted "Papi! Papi!"

Another fastball away, and another foul off the bat of Ortiz. The crowd exhaled again before once again taking a deep breath and raising the volume.

"Quite an at-bat by David Ortiz," O'Brien said. "I mean, I know he's had a lot of 'em, not only in this series but all season long for Boston, but this is something. It's almost as if he's determined not to let Loaiza put him away."

"How remarkable have these fans been here for Red Sox Nation tonight?" Sutcliffe asked. "Still standing. They've been standing since about the fifth inning."

"This has been a long, productive at-bat by Ortiz. He hopes to make it really productive, with a game-winning hit," Trupiano said.

Loaiza rubbed the baseball, preparing to deliver the tenth pitch of an absolutely epic at-bat. Ortiz dug in. The crowd noise reflected an uneasy energy, hoping to simply explode.

Loaiza came back inside with a cutter. Ortiz swung and, thanks to his prodigious strength, fought it off.

"Little blooper, center field! That drops down for a hit! Here comes Damon! He's in to score, and the Red Sox win it in fourteen innings! They're going to the Bronx!" O'Brien cried.

Fenway erupted. The Red Sox poured out of the dugout, some mobbing Damon at home and the rest mobbing Ortiz on the base path between first and second base. For the second straight night, the Red Sox kept their season alive in incredible extra-inning fashion against their archrivals.

"David Ortiz the magic man again," O'Brien said a minute later. "He won it with the homer in the twelfth last night, a game that ended at 1:22 this morning, so for the second time today, he's the hero with the game-winning hit."

"Ortiz, for the second night in a row, ends a game that lasts over five hours. This one took 14 innings, and you talk about earning your way back to New York, the Red Sox have earned a trip to Yankee Stadium for tomorrow night," Buck said, amidst a raucous Fenway celebration.

Neil Keefe, a Yankee fan attending the game, later wrote, "On the 10th pitch of the at-bat, he hit a line drive back up the middle, and sometimes when I close my eyes, I can still see it hanging in the air, wondering if Williams is going to get to it in time. He never does get to it in time, just like he didn't that night, and as Damon rounded third and headed for home, my heart sank. Damon touched home at 11:00 p.m.—five hours and forty-nine minutes after first pitch—in what was the longest postseason game in history at the time. I looked to my right where a fellow Yankees fan wearing a '1918' shirt stared out at the field in disbelief. I walked out of Fenway Park where Red Sox fans kindly let me know the result of the game as my emotional state was given away by my Yankees hat."

Gape Kapler, working for FOX years later, would say, "I'll tell you what I remember. With all due respect to Loaiza, I thought, 'This guy has nothing to get David out with.' That was the sentiment. And that wasn't unique to that at-bat. It's just because that was what was going on for David at that time."

Bill Simmons, in his unique style, chronicled his experience in that last moment: "By the time we were rallying again in the 14th, Francona needed to go to the bullpen for 35,000 new fans. We were spent. We were cooked. With Johnny D on second and Manny on first, with two outs and Hendu-Hobbs-Ghandi at the plate, we couldn't rise to the moment, not even when Big Papi kept fouling off those nasty pitches from Loaiza. Somewhere along the line, you could see him getting locked in again. He was right there.

"'Something's gonna happen here,' I remember telling Dad, who couldn't speak at this point.

"Something happened.

"A bloop hit into center field. The kind the Yankees always get. Johnny D rounded third with the winning run. Half the guys greeted him at home plate, half sprinted towards Ortiz. Then Johnny's group sprinted over to Ortiz for one giant jumpfest.

Meanwhile, you could see the Green Monster practically swaying. We were delirious—literally and figuratively—one of the happiest moments in the history of Fenway Park, right up there with Fisk's home run and everything else."

Somehow, some way, the Red Sox had staved off elimination *again*. They were dead and buried late in the game, with the Yankees' best pitchers on the mound, and they somehow came back to send it into extra innings. Once there, an unheralded group of pitchers, who had been mauled all series long by New York's thunderous lineup, kept the Yankees at bay, until Ortiz came through to win it.

They were indeed headed to New York for Game 6, after one of the most thrilling and tense games in baseball history.

POSTGAME

Both teams flew back to New York after the game, arriving in the wee hours of the morning on October 19. Both teams were exhausted, but there was no time to rest. Jon Lieber, who pitched seven innings of three-hit, one-run ball in a 3–1 Game 2 win over Pedro Martínez, once again pitched well. He pitched 7.1 innings in Game 6, allowing nine hits and four runs, all of them in the Boston half of the fourth inning. Boston had him in trouble in the second, but Bellhorn grounded into a bases-loaded double play to allow Lieber to escape. In the fourth, Boston produced some two-out magic. Millar doubled, Varitek singled him in, Cabrera singled, and then Bellhorn hit a low line drive that barely cleared the fence in left field for a three-run homer.

At first, the umps ruled it a double, as the ball looked like it may have hit the top of the fence. There was no replay rule then, so the umps got together to talk. Replay (the umps couldn't use it but the fans watching could see) showed that the ball clearly cleared the fence and hit off a fan before bouncing back into the field of play. They ruled it a home run, and Boston had a four-run lead.

Schilling, pitching on a badly damaged right ankle that required a novel surgical procedure to hold it together, threw six shutout innings with his ankle leaking blood. His bloody sock is in the Hall of Fame. In the seventh, he gave up a Bernie Williams home run, but that's all. He finished seven incredibly gutsy innings, allowing just four hits and the lone run.

In the eighth, New York staged a rally. Jeter (who else?) singled in Cairo off Bronson Arroyo, and then Rodriguez hit a tiny grounder down the first base line. Arroyo fielded it, tagged Rodriguez, but the ball came out. Jeter came all the way around to score, and A-Rod made it to second. New York, down just a run, had momentum, and Yankee Stadium was rocking. But once again, the umpires got together and ruled that, in fact, Rodriguez chopped down on Arroyo's arm, and that's why the ball came out. They infamously changed the ruling to interference and called Rodriguez out and sent Jeter back to first. The Yankee crowd, incensed, began to throw debris on the field. Francona wanted his team cleared off the field, hoping for things to settle down. He didn't want any of his players hit with bottles or baseballs thrown from the stands. Yankee fans knew things were unraveling.

A-Rod stood at second, pleading his case, pretending that he "accidentally" hit Arroyo's arm in the process of running. The announcers were all over it, pointing out how obvious it was that he slapped down to knock the ball free. Crew chief Joe West, who correctly made the ruling on the Bellhorn homer, stood firm and got this one right as well.

Arroyo got out of the inning by getting Sheffield to pop-up. But in the ninth, with Foulke on again, pitching hugely stressful innings for Boston for the third night in a row, he walked Matsui and Sierra and, with two out, faced Tony Clark. The count went full, and Foulke finally threw a fastball past Clark, who swung and missed to end the game, with Boston winning 4–2.

Simmons wrote, "The classic move would be for the Sox to win three games in a row, then lose the climactic seventh game. But this isn't a classic Red Sox team. The old Red Sox would have blown game four or game five, and they definitely would have choked away game six. With the old Red Sox, Bellhorn's homer gets ruled a double, A-Rod definitely gets called safe at first base, and Cairo [he meant Clark] clears the bases for the game winner in the ninth. Here's the point: Those things haven't been happening. Sometimes you pass a point where history becomes a factor, like with the Patriots three years ago when the diehards kept waiting for The Other Shoe to drop, and we were waiting and waiting, and suddenly Vinatieri's final kick split the uprights, the most liberating feeling you can imagine. That's the thing about baggage as a sports fan—you can shed this stuff. You just need a few breaks. This Boston team is getting them."

Game 7 was started by Derek Lowe, working on two days' rest, and Kevin Brown. The Yankees brought out all the stops, as it was played on Mickey Mantle's birthday, and they had Bucky Dent, of all people, throw out the first pitch. It didn't matter. Boston jumped all over Brown in the first, with Ortiz hitting a two-run homer. Damon's bat finally came alive, with a first-inning single, followed by a second-inning grand slam to put Boston up 6–0. Arroyo allowed a run in the third but quelled a Yankee rally, and in the top of the fourth, Damon hit another homer, and just like that, Boston led 8–1.

Loaiza came on to pitch three more quality innings for New York, but they couldn't score off Lowe. In the seventh, in one of the more curious moves all postseason, Francona invited disaster by bringing in Pedro Martínez in relief, perhaps a sentimental decision given Pedro's struggles during the series. It was just what the Yankee crowd needed to spark them, and the fans roared with, "Who's your daddy!?" chants. New York promptly scored twice off Martínez, but he got John Olerud and Miguel Cairo to end the inning, leaving with a five-run lead.

In the eighth, Bellhorn, whose homer won Game 6, homered again, a perfect response to the Yankee runs in the seventh. In the ninth, Cabrera drove in Trot Nixon with a sacrifice fly, and Timlin and Embree then combined to end the game. The last out of the series came on a slow grounder to second baseman Pokey Reese, who calmly threw Rubén Sierra out, and Boston celebrated an unprecedented pennant on the hallowed grounds of Yankee Stadium with a 10–3 whipping of the Yankees.

SIMMONS SUMMED IT up, "You have to be a Red Sox fan to understand. You just do. It wasn't just that the Yankees always win. It was everything else that came with it—the petty barbs, the condescending remarks, the general sense of superiority from a fan base that derives a disproportionate amount of self-esteem from the success of their baseball team. I didn't care that they kept winning as much as that they were assholes about it. Not all of them. Some of them. In 96 hours, everything was erased. Everything. It was like pressing the reset button on a video game. And yeah, I know. We need to win the World Series to complete the dream. But you can win the World Series any year; you only have one chance to destroy the Yanks."

In the World Series, Boston won a wild Game 1, 11–9, and they then proceeded to simply suffocate the Cardinals, who had won 105 games during the season. Boston got big home runs, timely defensive plays, and terrific pitching. Schilling was great in Game 2. Pedro was brilliant in Game 3 with seven shutout innings in his final start as a member of the Boston Red Sox. Lowe once again won the final game of a series—the third straight post-season series he achieved that—and Boston won its first World Series since 1918.

Joe Castiglione on WEEI called the historic final out: "Swing and a ground ball, stabbed by Foulke. He has it…he underhands to first…and the Boston Red Sox are World Champions! For the first time in eighty-six years the Boston Red Sox have won baseball's world championship! Can you believe it!?"

Boston was good in 2005, winning 95 games, but was bounced in the divisional series by a White Sox team on a mission. Chicago went on to win the World Series in dominating fashion. In 2006, Boston slipped to an 86-win season and they missed the playoffs. Needed moves were made, and they were, and they came back strong in 2007 behind the right arm of Josh Beckett (20–7, 3.27 ERA) and the bat of David Ortiz (.332, 38 homers, 117 RBIs). In the ALCS, they were down three games to one against Cleveland but rallied to win three straight and clinch the pennant. After 2004's epic comeback against New York, being down three games to one seemed like a very doable task. In the World Series, they overwhelmed a Colorado Rockies team that had won 21 of their last 22 games, including sweeps of the Phillies and Diamondbacks in the NL playoffs. Boston swept Colorado in four straight, bringing their World Series winning streak to eight straight games.

Boston won 95 games in 2008 and made it to the ALCS, losing in seven games to the Tampa Bay Rays. However, 95 more wins in 2009 produced a disappointing loss to the Angels in three straight games in the divisional round, and the Yankees won the World Series.

Boston would struggle the next two seasons, finishing in third both times (Francona would be fired after the 2011 season), and 2012 was a 69-win disaster under new manager Bobby Valentine. But then came 2013, with John Farrell at the helm, and Boston, a team filled with exciting youngsters and veterans having special seasons, rolled to 97 wins, a dramatic victory over Detroit in the ALCS, and then a thrilling six-game victory over the Cardinals in the World Series. Ortiz had one of the greatest World Series performances of all time, and veteran closer Koji Uehara was virtually unhittable. Boston won for the first time at home since 1918.

The Red Sox then found themselves in the wilderness for a couple of seasons before winning 93 games in 2016 and 2017, but both seasons resulted in first-round playoff exits. For David Ortiz, his final season came in 2016 at the age of forty. He left the game still performing at an elite level, hitting .315, with a .401 OBP, 1.021 OPS, 38 homers, 48 doubles, and 127 RBIs. He retired after that year, citing the wear and tear on his aging body.

2018 produced the greatest season any Red Sox team ever fielded. Ace starter Chris Sale led the pitching staff. Mookie Betts, a rookie in 2014, won the MVP hitting .346 with 32 homers and 30 stolen bases. Boston won 108 games and steamrolled through the playoffs, beating 100-win New York, 103-win Houston, and the defending NL champion Dodgers in succession to win their fourth World Series of the century, more than any other team in baseball.

NONE OF THIS would have been possible without Game 5 of the 2004 ALCS. The courage, the fortitude, the willingness to stick to it and not give an inch on that chilly October night, both for Boston and New York, was remarkable. Game 4 was the Dave Roberts game. Game 6 was the Bloody Sock game. Game 7 was the game where Boston finally vanquished the Yankees and completed the greatest comeback in baseball history.

But Game 5 was maybe the best, most tense, most thrilling, most exhausting baseball game in Red Sox history.

NOTES

The table on the following page shows the relevant statistics comparing the great pitchers discussed in Chapter 5: Walter Johnson, Grover Cleveland Alexander, Christy Mathewson, Sandy Koufax, Mordecai "Three Finger" Brown, Cy Young, Greg Maddux, Randy Johnson, Tom Seaver, Lefty Grove, Roger Clemens, Tim Keefe, Bob Gibson, Clayton Kershaw, Warren Spahn, Mariano Rivera, and Pedro Martínez.

Table 1: Four Year Peak

Pitcher	Years	Innings	W-L	ERA	ERA+	Best ERA+	WHIP	K/9
Alexander	1915–1918	1179.1	96–36	1.54	178	225	0.94	4.8
Brown	1906–1909	1165.1	102–30	1.31	191	253	0.89	4.2
Clemens	1989–1992	999.2	74–38	2.54	165	211	1.10	8.0
Gibson	1966–1969	1074.1	76–41	2.08	161	258	1.01	7.6
Grove	1928–1931	1116.2	103–23	2.49	175	217	1.16	5.9
R Johnson	1999–2002	1030.0	81–27	2.48	187	195	1.04	12.4
W Johnson	1912–1915	1423.1	124–50	1.45	209	259	0.90	6.2
Keefe	1885–1888	1846.0	144–64	2.30	136	174	1.04	5.1
Kershaw	2013–2016	816.0	65–23	1.88	195	197	0.86	10.4
Koufax	1963–1966	1192.2	97–27	1.86	172	190	0.91	9.3
Maddux	1992–1995	946.2	75–29	1.98	202	271	0.95	7.0
Martínez	1999–2002	746.1	68–17	2.07	233	291	0.87	12.0
Mathewson	1908–1911	1291.1	115–39	1.62	174	233	0.96	5.1
Seaver	1968–1971	1128.1	79–41	2.25	157	194	1.01	7.9
Spahn	1951–1954	1149.2	80–52	2.82	133	188	1.18	4.9
Rivera	2003–2006	302.2	21–13	1.69	261	308	0.98	7.9
Young	1901–1904	1477.2	119–46	1.96	164	219	0.98	4.2

REFERENCES

John Snyder. "2004 ALCS Game 5: Yankees @ Red Sox (Fox Broadcast)." November 5, 2017. Youtube video, 4:40:31. https://www.youtube.com /watch?v=AbokSfoNZyQ&t=2068s

MLB Vault. "2004 ALCS, Game 5: Yankees @ Red Sox." September 21, 2010. Youtube video, 4:57:35. https://www.youtube.com/watch?v= 4Ttjci5KPQo&t=2666s

Bill Simmons, *Now I Can Die in Peace* (Connecticut: ESPN Books, 2005).

Tim McCarver, *Tim McCarver's Baseball for Brain Surgeons and Other Fans: Understanding and Interpreting the Game So You Can Watch It Like a Pro* (New York: Random House Publishing Group, 2013).

Every player in the game's Wiki page—https://www.wikipedia.org

Every player in the game's Baseball Reference page—https://www.baseball-reference.com

Mike Dyer, "How NBC captured Carlton Fisk's home run in the 1975 World Series," Cincinnati.com, last modified October 21, 2015, https://www.cincinnati.com/story/sports/2015/10/21/remembering -game-6-of-the-1975-world-series/74319024/

Elliott Almond and Mike Penner, "Donnie Moore Dies in Apparent Suicide: Home Run Pitch in 1986 Playoffs Haunted Moore, Says His Agent," *Los Angeles Times*, July 19, 1989, https://www.latimes.com/ archives/la-xpm-1989-07-19-sp-3894-story.html

NBC Sports Boston Staff, "Doug Mirabelli got a police escort to Fenway Park 13 years ago today," NBC Sports, May 1, 2019, https://www.nbcsports.com/boston/red-sox/doug-mirabelli-got-police-escort-fenway-park-13-years-ago-today

Sam Gardner, "The Night the Legend of David Ortiz Took Off," FOX Sports, October 6, 2016, https://www.foxsports.com/stories/mlb/the-night-the-legend-of-david-ortiz-took-off

Nathaniel Rakich, "Manny Ramirez, Steroids, and Having it Both Ways in the Hall of Fame," VICE, January 17, 2017, https://www.vice.com/en_us/article/8qy5mb/manny-ramirez-steroids-and-having-it-both-ways-in-the-hall-of-fame

Ben Buchanan, "For Manny Ramirez more than most, steroids stands in the way of Hall of Fame," Over The Monster, November 22, 2016, https://www.overthemonster.com/2016/11/22/13715066/for-manny-ramirez-more-than-most-steroids-stand-in-the-way-of-hall-of

J. J. Cooper, "How Many MLB Draftees Make It To The Majors," Baseball America, May 17, 2019, https://www.baseballamerica.com/stories/how-many-mlb-draftees-make-it-to-the-majors/

"Catching a Knuckleball for the BoSox," NPR, May 2, 2006, https://www.npr.org/templates/story/story.php?storyId=5377333

Ken Rosenthal, "The Art of Knuckleball Catching," FOX Sports, April 1, 2015, https://www.foxsports.com/stories/mlb/the-art-of-knuckleball-catching

ESPN.com news services, "Francona bets Lucchino he can quit tobacco habit," ESPN, March 1, 2007, https://www.espn.com/mlb/spring2007/news/story?id=2784137

A Farmer, "An Ode to Knuckleball Pitchers," Letters from a Farmer in Ohio, March 9, 2011, http://afarmerinohio.blogspot.com/2011/03/ode-to-knuckleball-pitchers.html

"Comments on the K-ball," Oddball-mall, http://www.oddball-mall.com/knuckleball/quotes.htm

"Knuckleball Quotes," AZ Quotes, https://www.azquotes.com/quotes/topics/knuckleballs.html

"Knuckleball," Wikipedia, last modified January 27, 2021. https://en.wikipedia.org/wiki/Knuckleball

REFERENCES

"Tim Wakefield," Wikipedia, last modified January 27, 2021 https:// en.wikipedia.org/wiki/Tim_Wakefield

Mark Patinkin, "A towering talent from the lowliest of starts," *Providence Journal*, last modified October 16, 2016, https://www.providence-journal.com/news/20161015/mark-patinkin-towering-talent-from -lowliest-of-starts

Baseball-reference.com

"Indians' Francona Visits Dentist at 1 A.M. After Losing Tooth in ALCS," CBS New York, October 18, 2016, https://newyork.cbslocal. com/2016/10/18/indians-terry-francona-loses-tooth/

Kenny Ducey, "Terry Francona lost a tooth during Game 3, and had it put back in at 1 a.m.," *Sports Illustrated*, October 18, 2016, https://www. si.com/extra-mustard/2016/10/18/terry-francona-lost-tooth-alcs -game-3-tobacco

Saul Wisnia, "The One Annoying Thing About Indians Manager Terry Francona," Bleacher Report, May 27, 2013, https://bleacherreport. com/articles/1653611-the-one-annoying-thing-about-indians-man-ager-terry-francona

Bob Nightengale, "Baseball tested Terry Francona's health, but game 'almost killed me when it was taken away,'" *USA Today*, last modified July 20, 2017,https://www.usatoday.com/story/sports/mlb/2017/07/20/ indians-manager-terry-francona-heart-illness-return/495105001/

"NY Yankees 1996 salaries," *USA Today*, https://www.usatoday.com/sports /mlb/yankees/salaries/1996/player/all/

Joe Posnanski, "Save evolves from stat to game changer," MLB.com, April 12, 2017, https://www.mlb.com/news/how-save-rule-has-changed -baseball-c223677902

Fran Zimniuch, *Fireman: The Evolution of the Closer in Baseball* (Chicago: Triumph Books, 2010), https://archive.org/details/firemanevolution 0000zimn/page/154/mode/2up

"Setup man," Wikipedia, last modified January 2, 2021, https://en.wiki-pedia.org/wiki/Setup_man

"Save (SV)," MLB.com, http://m.mlb.com/glossary/standard-stats/save

Ian Browne, "Ortiz's heroics, Nixon's grab kept '04 WS in sight," MLB.com, October 18, 2014, https://www.mlb.com/news/david-ortizs-heroics -trot-nixons-grab-kept-2004-ws-in-sight-for-red-sox/c-98920062

Chad Finn, "Retro Recap, 2004 ALCS Game 5: Another Papi Walkoff, and the Best Game of Varitek's Life," Boston.com, http://archive.boston.com/sports/touching_all_the_bases/2014/10/retro_recap_2004_alcs_game_5.html

Mike Cole, "Red Sox Encore : Relive Sox-Yankees 2004 ALCS Game 5 Before NESN Broadcast," NESN, May 1, 2020, https://nesn.com/2020/05/red-sox-encore-relive-sox-yankees-2004-alcs-game-5-before-nesn-broadcast/

Tyler Kepner, "Even Longer: Red Sox Win Game 5 in 14 Innings," *The New York Times*, October 19, 2004, https://www.nytimes.com/2004/10/19/sports/baseball/even-longer-red-sox-win-game-5-in-14-innings.html

Neil Keefe, "Game 5 of the 2004 ALCS," Keefe to the City, January 1, 2020, http://keefetothecity.com/game-5-of-the-2004-alcs/

"Boston Marathon bombing," Wikipedia, last modified February 25, 2021, https://en.wikipedia.org/wiki/Boston_Marathon_bombing

Joel Reuter, "The 5 Most Clutch Postseason Players in Every Baseball Era," Bleacher Report, October 10, 2011, https://bleacherreport.com/articles/886079-the-5-most-clutch-postseason-players-in-every-baseball-ERA

Nate Silver, *Baseball Between the Numbers: Why Everything You Know About the Game is Wrong* (New York: Basic Books, 2006) https://www.espn.com/espn/page2/story?page=betweenthenumbers/ortiz/060405

Jack Bardsley, "Why David Ortiz Is The Greatest Clutch Hitter In Baseball History," Boston's Big Four, May 15, 2016, https://www.bostonsbigfour.com/why-david-ortiz-is-the-greatest-clutch-hitter-in-baseball-history/

Peter Weber, "Why the FCC isn't upset about David Ortiz's Boston Red Sox F-bomb," *The Week*, April 22, 2013, https://theweek.com/articles/465276/why-fcc-isnt-upset-about-david-ortizs-boston-red-sox-fbomb

Dave D'Onofrio, "13 moments when David Ortiz defined clutch," Boston.com, November 8, 2016, https://www.boston.com/sports/boston-red-sox/2016/11/08/when-david-ortiz-defined-clutch

Jim Baumbach, "Setup Became Upset," *Newsday*, February 24, 2005, https://www.newsday.com/sports/setup-became-upset-1.501746

REFERENCES

Andrew Kyne, "The Effectiveness of 'Infield In' Defense," Sports Info Solutions, May 3, 2019, http://www.sportsinfosolutions.com/the-effectiveness-of-infield-in-defense/

Randy Leonard, "Baseball's Long and Complicated Relationship With the Bunt," *The Atlantic*, October 1, 2014, https://www.theatlantic.com/entertainment/archive/2014/10/baseballs-long-and-complicated-relationship-with-the-bunt/380563/

Tom Tango, "Tango on Baseball," Tangotiger.net, 2008, http://www.tangotiger.net

Dan Blewett, "Run Expectancy And Why Bunting Is Bad," Danblewett.com, last modified March 8, 2020, https://danblewett.com/run-expectancy-bunting-bad/

"David Ortiz," Wikipedia, last modified February 20, 2021, https://en.wikipedia.org/wiki/David_Ortiz

Larry Brooks, "Sox Sit In Crosshairs," *New York Post*, April 3, 2005, https://nypost.com/2005/04/03/sox-sit-in-crosshairs/

David Heuschkel, "Red Sox: Amid The Bluster, Voices Of Reason," *Hartford Courant*, July 14, 2005, https://www.courant.com/news/connecticut/hc-xpm-2005-07-14-0507140678-story.html

Matthew Kory, "Ten Revelations From Terry Francona's New Book," Over The Monster, January 17, 2013, https://www.overthemonster.com/2013/1/17/3885868/ten-revelations-boston-red-sox-terry-francona-new-book

"Remarks Honoring the 2007 World Series Champion Boston Red Sox," The American Presidency Project, February 27, 2008. https://www.presidency.ucsb.edu/documents/remarks-honoring-the-2007-world-series-champion-boston-red-sox

Dan Flaherty, "The 2004 Boston Red Sox Make History," The Sports Notebook, October 25, 2018, https://thesportsnotebook.com/2004-boston-red-sox-sports-history-articles/

"2004 Boston Red Sox season," Wikipedia, last modified January 20, 2021, https://en.wikipedia.org/wiki/2004_Boston_Red_Sox_season

Bill Chuck, "Pedro Martinez's peak stats are even better than you remember," Boston.com, July 25, 2015, https://www.boston.com/sports/boston-red-sox/2015/07/25/pedro-martinezs-peak-stats-are-even-better-than-you-remember

Tim Kurkjian, "Tim Kurkjian's Baseball Fix: Roger Clemens was a power pitcher, from start to finish," ESPN, May 20, 2020, https://www.espn.com/mlb/story/_/id/29160691/tim-kurkjian-baseball-fix-roger-clemens-was-power-pitcher-start-finish

Sam Miller, "Hunches, home runs and humiliation: Nine tales of unsung World Series heroes," ESPN, May 20, 2020, https://www.espn.com/mlb/story/_/id/29142113/mlb-nine-tales-unsung-world-series-heroes

Jay Boice, "How Our 2016 MLB Predictions Work," FiveThirtyEight, April 25, 2016, https://fivethirtyeight.com/features/how-our-2016-mlb-predictions-work/

Jeff Angus, "Does 'Game Score' Still Work in Today's High-Offense Game?," SABR, 2010, https://sabr.org/research/does-game-score-still-work-today-s-high-offense-game

"Game score," Wikipedia, last modified October 24, 2020, https://en.wikipedia.org/wiki/Game_score

"The Steroids ERA," ESPN, December 5, 2012, http://www.espn.com/mlb/topics/_/page/the-steroids-ERA

Ed Graney, "Peers explain what made Maddux smartest pitcher ever," Las Vegas Review-Journal, July 27, 2014, https://www.reviewjournal.com/sports/sports-columns/ed-graney/peers-explain-what-made-maddux-smartest-pitcher-ever/

Jeff Sullivan, "An Inning with Greg Maddux," FanGraphs, January 24, 2014, https://blogs.fangraphs.com/an-inning-with-greg-madduxs-command/

Joe Posnanski, "Introducing 'The Maddux' to its legendary namesake," MLB.com, May 9, 2017, https://www.mlb.com/news/greg-maddux-was-master-of-control-efficiency-c229043154

"Dead-ball era," Wikipedia, last modified February 11, 2021, https://en.wikipedia.org/wiki/Dead-ball_era

Clint Davis, "The Best Pitchers In MLB History," The Delite, February 12, 2020, https://www.thedelite.com/greatest-pitchers-mlb-history/

Neil Paine and Jay Boice, "The Best Pitchers Of All Time," FiveThirtyEight, May 12, 2016, https://fivethirtyeight.com/features/the-best-pitchers-of-all-time/

REFERENCES

Nicholas Ian Allen, "25 Best Starting Pitchers of All Time," Athlon Sports, April 20, 2017, https://athlonsports.com/mlb/25-greatest-starting-pitchers-major-league-baseball-history

jorgenswest, "Third Time Through The Order: Established Knowledge or Statistical Illusion?," Twins Daily, September 08, 2018, http://twinsdaily.com/blog/36/entry-11217-third-time-through-the-order-established-knowledge-or-statistical-illusion/

David Waldstein, "Stubbornness, as Much as Skill, Kept Derek Jeter on Top," The New York Times, January 21, 2020, https://www.nytimes.com/2020/01/21/sports/baseball/jeter-hall-of-fame-yankees.html

Tyler Kepner, "BASEBALL; Yanks Assure Jeter He's Safe At Shortstop," The New York Times, February 17, 2004, https://www.nytimes.com/2004/02/17/sports/baseball-yanks-assure-jeter-he-s-safe-at-shortstop.html

Tom Verducci, "Hello, New York," Sports Illustrated, February 23, 2004, https://vault.si.com/vault/2004/02/23/hello-new-york-by-agreeing-to-move-to-third-base-alex-rodriguez-got-out-of-texas-and-into-pinstripes-as-the-yankees-pulled-off-another-blockbuster

Ryan Bort, "A Brief History of Derek Jeter and Alex Rodriguez's Roller Coaster Relationship," Newsweek, May, 11, 2017, https://www.newsweek.com/alex-rodriguez-derek-jeter-history-607464

Dan Holmes, "Was Jeter better than Nomar and ARod?," Baseball Egg, February 15, 2018, http://baseballegg.com/2018/02/15/was-jeter-better-than-nomar-and-arod/

Ken Davidoff, "Yanks' Position: All Is Well/A-Rod aboard, but Jeter is still shortstop," Newsday, February 16, 2004, https://www.newsday.com/sports/yanks-position-all-is-well-a-rod-aboard-but-jeter-is-still-shortstop-1.705194

Chris Mitchell, "Why did the Yankees keep Jeter at shortstop?," SB Nation, August 6, 2014 https://www.pinstripealley.com/yankees-analysis-sabermetrics/2014/8/6/5973413/yankees-jeter-shortstop-defense-rodriguez

Eoin Higgins, "Jeter, Not A-Rod, Was the Selfish One," Eoinhiggins.com, August 12, 2016, https://eoinhiggins.com/jeter-not-a-rod-was-the-selfish-one-ec02a559b1dc

"Nippon Professional Baseball Organization," http://npb.jp/eng/

Tyler Kepner, "BASEBALL; Matsui and Yankees Agree to a Deal," *The New York Times*, December 20, 2002, https://www.nytimes.com/2002/12/20/sports/baseball-matsui-and-yankees-agree-to-a-deal.html

Adam Dorhauer, "Baseball ProGUESTus: On Runs, Wins, and Two Types of Leverage Index," Baseball Prospectus, March 13, 2012, https://www.baseballprospectus.com/news/article/16212/baseball-proguestus-on-runs-wins-and-two-types-of-leverage-index/

"Leverage Index," MLB.com, http://m.mlb.com/glossary/advanced-stats/leverage-index

Tom M. Tango, "Crucial Situations," *The Hardball Times*, May 1, 2006, https://tht.fangraphs.com/crucial-situations/

Tangotiger, "Leverage Index," InsideTheBook.com, http://www.insidethebook.com/li.shtml

Steve Slowinski, "LI," FanGraphs, February 17, 2010, https://library.fangraphs.com/misc/li/

Dave Allen, "Hot Stove U: Stress Pitches vs. Pitch Count," FanGraphs, February 24, 2010, https://plus.fangraphs.com/hot-stove-u-stress-pitches-vs-pitch-count/

David Manel, "A new tool for measuring pitcher stress," SB Nation, September 16, 2015, https://www.bucsdugout.com/2015/9/16/9334433/mlb-pitcher-stress-index

RJ Loubier, "On this day in Yankee history—Game 7 of the 2003 ALCS," Bronx Pinstripes, October 16, 2003, http://bronxpinstripes.com/yankees-history/game-7-of-the-2003-alcs/

Jay Jaffe, "Despite steroids scandals, retiring Giambi rebuilt his reputation," *Sports Illustrated*, February 17, 2015, https://www.si.com/mlb/2015/02/17/jason-giambi-retires-yankees-athletics-rockies-indians

Gordon Edes, "Thumb's down: Reese, Red Sox fall," Boston.com, June 24, 2004, http://archive.boston.com/sports/baseball/redsox/articles/2004/06/24/thumbs_down_reese_red_sox_fall/

Associated Press, "Injuries Sideline Nixon, Garciaparra," *The Los Angeles Times*, March 20, 2004, https://www.latimes.com/archives/la-xpm-2004-mar-20-sp-bbnotes20-story.html

"Red Sox Encore: Relive Sox-Yankees 2004 ALCS Game 5 Before NESN Broadcast," News Break, https://www.newsbreak.com/massachusetts/boston/news/0OvlJLdT/red-sox-encore-relive-sox-yankees-2004-alcs-game-5-before-nesn-broadcast

Bill Simmons, "The surreal life at Fenway," ESPN.com, https://www.espn.com/espn/page2/story?page=simmons/041019

"Walk(off) this way!," *Boston Herald*, August 11, 2013, https://www.bostonherald.com/2013/08/11/walkoff-this-way/

Lauren Campbell, "Red Sox Legend Pedro Martinez Opens Up About 2004 ALCS, 'Daddy' Comment," NESN, September 24, 2019, https://nesn.com/2019/09/red-sox-legend-pedro-martinez-opens-up-about-2003-alcs-daddy-comment/

Sean Sylver, "Ten Years Gone: Pedro Martinez calls the Yankees his daddy," Bosox Injection, September 24, 2014, https://bosoxinjection.com/2014/09/24/ten-years-gone-pedro-martinez-calls-yankees-daddy/

Matt Snyder, "Happy 10th Anniversary: Pedro Martinez calls Yankees his 'Daddy,'" CBS Sports, September 24, 2014, https://www.cbssports.com/mlb/news/happy-10th-anniversary-pedro-martinez-calls-yankees-his-daddy/

"List of American League Championship Series broadcasters," Wikipedia, last modified February 16, 2021, https://en.wikipedia.org/wiki/List_of_American_League_Championship_Series_broadcasters

Joel Sherman, "Inside the complex trade that brought A-Rod to the Yankees," *New York Post*, February 15, 2014, https://nypost.com/2014/02/15/how-a-rod-landed-with-yanks-10-years-ago-is-a-complex-tale/

Tim Boyle, "Grade the Trade: Rangers trade Alex Rodriguez to the Yankees for Alfonso Soriano," Fansided, October 28, 2017, https://calltothepen.com/2017/10/28/grade-the-trade-rangers-trade-alex-rodriguez-to-the-yankees-for-alfonso-soriano/

Ben Nicholson-Smith, "Trades Of The Decade: A-Rod For Soriano," MLB Trade Rumors, November 26, 2009, https://www.mlbtraderumors.com/2009/11/trades-of-the-decade-arod-for-soriano.html

Jack Curry, "BASEBALL; Red Sox Draw Line, and Yankees Cross It," *The New York Times*, February 19, 2004, https://www.nytimes.com/2004/02/19/sports/baseball-red-sox-draw-line-and-yankees-cross-it.html

"Alex Rodriguez explains why he wanted to join the Red Sox (not Yankees) in 2003," Boston Sports, December 5, 2018. https://www.nbcsports. com/boston/red-sox/alex-rodriguez-explains-why-he-wanted-join-red-sox-not-yankees-2003

NESN Staff, "*Theo Epstein Pulls Curtain Back On Failed Alex Rodriguez-To-Red Sox Trade*," *NESN*, April 2, 2017, https://nesn.com/2017 /04/theo-epstein-pulls-curtain-back-on-failed-alex-rodriguez-to-red-sox-trade/

"The Turning Point: When The Sox Won Game Four Against The Yankees," Radio Boston, April 16, 2012, https://www.wbur.org/radioboston /2012/04/16/red-sox-game-four

Grant Brisbee, "A brief history of teams down 0-3 in a best-of-seven series," SB Nation, last modified October 21, 2015, https://www. sbnation.com/mlb/2014/10/15/6983961/orioles-royals-alcs -teams-down-0-3-playoffs-postseason-baseball

A brief history of teams down 0–3 in a best of seven series. https://www.wbur. org/radioboston/2012/04/16/red-sox-game-four

David Schoenfield, "The Red Sox begin amazing comeback," ESPN.com, December 14, 2009, http://www.espn.com/espn/page2/story?page= games/decade/2004alcs

ACKNOWLEDGMENTS

It's one thing to be a baseball fan. It's another to have the privilege of writing a book about a sport you have loved since childhood. I remember my first visit to Fenway Park as a boy. It was August 29, 1978. Boston played Seattle, and my family joined my buddy Matt's family for what would become an annual tradition—several days in Boston for a vacation, which included stops at the Museum of Science, the Aquarium, Quincy's Market, and of course, a baseball game at Fenway.

It was a warm evening, and we sat down the left field line, a whole group of us. The sensation coming out of the tunnel and seeing the ballpark was surreal. Glorious green grass. Bright white lines. The Green Monster looming near us off to our left. The sounds and smells of the ballpark overwhelmed me.

A man behind us proceeded to enjoy a ballpark tradition in Boston (and elsewhere)—he got completely hammered. And knowing that it was our first time in Fenway, he helped us celebrate by buying us slices of pizza, hot dogs, popcorn, and pretty much anything else we wanted.

In the fifth inning, Red Sox' first baseman George "Boomer" Scott launched a grand slam right past us, over the Monster, giving us first-timers quite the thrill. The next time he came up, I unwisely bet Matt a dime that the Mariners would walk Scott intentionally. They didn't, and I didn't have a dime to pay up. My father covered my debt and I learned at that point to never again bet on sports. The Red Sox went on to win 10–5, the first of many incredible memories at baseball stadiums.

Since then, I have seen Roger Clemens dominate hitters in Fenway, and I recall the first time I saw him pitch. I was sitting in the right field stands and the unreal popping sound of his fastball hitting the catcher's mitt, some 400 feet away, still resonates. I saw the Yankees and Red Sox on a day when I was dreadfully sick upon arrival and spent the first two innings in the bathroom. When I emerged, I was a new person, and I think my recovery helped the Red Sox come back to beat the Yankees. I saw Cleveland beat Pedro Martínez with my then coworker Nate. I saw Mike Mussina beat Pedro in Yankee Stadium just months before the horrific 9/11 attacks. I visited Yankee Stadium on August 3, 2010 with my sons, my father, my Aunt Irene, and my cousin Kim (the latter three of whom are all die-hard Yankee fans) to see the Blue Jays beat New York 8–2. It was the day before Alex Rodriguez hit his six-hundredth career homer.

This book would not exist without my love for baseball, which was birthed and fostered by my father. Dad, thank you for teaching me the game, for coaching me in Little League, for bringing me to the ballpark often, and for continuing to talk with me over the years about everything related to baseball. I'm sorry I hung up on you when Jorge Posada hit the tying double off Pedro Martínez in the bottom of the eighth in Game 7 of the 2003 ALCS.

My wife, Diane, has had to put up with my love for baseball as well. Our boys played baseball for years, and she spent countless days and nights watching me coach and them play, becoming a baseball mom—something she never really imagined before we got married. My friend Matt's advice to Diane the night before our wedding was this: "You'd better love baseball, because John sure does." When the Red Sox won the World Series in 2004, after an eighty-six-year drought, she looked at me in the moments following the final out and asked, "Was it worth the wait?" I smiled and answered, "Yes." Thanks for loving me so well through these years and through this process, Di.

I am grateful for friends like Gar Ryness and Scott Cordischi, who looked this over and gave me feedback. I am indebted to people I have met through Sons of Sam Horn, a Red Sox (and other Boston sports) fan site, who have helped make my love for, and knowledge of, the game grow. In particular, I'd like to thank Commander Dan Withers (US Navy, Ret.), Mike Sherman, Ryan Siever, and Terry Nau for reviewing the book and helping me make it sharper. I'm also thankful for my old college buddy Stephen Loeb, who gave me important legal advice on this project, as well as my friends who are already published authors, for giving me guidance along the way.

Finally, I would like to thank my agent, Amanda Luedeke, who has worked tirelessly on my behalf to help get this book to print. Amanda, you're a wonderful agent and I cannot sing your praises enough.

ABOUT THE AUTHOR

John Vampatella graduated from Syracuse University in 1991 with a Bachelor of Science degree, majoring in Broadcast Journalism from the S.I. Newhouse School of Public Communication. He is currently the Northeast Regional Director with Athletes in Action.